BORDERLINE PERSONALITY DISORDER

BEING COMFORTABLE IN YOUR OWN SKIN

Simple Ways To Fight and Win Against BPD With Proven Cognitive Behavioral Therapy

Aden Garner

1

What Is Borderline Personality Disorder

Borderline personality disorder is an extremely serious mental disorder of impulsive actions and usually has a chain of unstable relationships. You can see the disorder with marks of ongoing mood instabilities and other instabilities such as behavior, self-image, and function. The person with BPD has very high anger, depression, and anxiety episodes that can last from a few hours to a few days. You can have BPD in correlation to having mood disorders, anxiety disorders, eating disorders, substance abuse, self-harm, suicidal thoughts, and suicide. Most medical professionals will agree with each other on the fact that the name "Borderline Personality Disorder" is misleading to the average citizen, but sadly a more accurate term does not exist yet.

There are many signs and symptoms of people with BPD, the most common that you will see is extreme mood swings. You can also see efforts to escape or avoid real abandonment or imagined abandonment. An unusual pattern of unstable relationships with your friends and family. It can sway from extreme closeness and love to hatred and anger. You will see them having a wrongly portrayed version of themselves or their self-image. You will also see many reckless behaviors such as spending outrageous amounts of money, abuse of substances, driving recklessly, and binging. Cutting and suicidal thoughts also show up in people with borderline personality disorder. Mood changes are regular with mood swings that last for a few hours to a few days. Many people with BPD observe a strong feeling of emptiness, uncontrollable anger, inappropriate comments, and having stress-related paranoid thoughts. Most people also feel cut off from themselves, as if they are observing themselves from outside of the body and slowly losing touch with reality. Any of these symptoms can be triggered by the minuscule events.

People with borderline personality disorder can see the anger in others while they are showing a neutral face and can also hear the anger in people's words more usually than people without BPD. Some of the symptoms above can also be traced back to other mental issues, and to people who don't have any mental issues, so do not just assume someone around you have this disorder and go get a doctor's diagnosis. A suitable medical professional needs to do a thorough assessment to see what outcome is appropriate.

Borderline personality disorder affects 5.9% of adults during one stage of their life. That equates to about 14 million Americans having BPD. You can see a connection of mental disorders within the patients with multiple diagnoses. About half of the people with Alzheimer's disease have borderline personality disorder. With others, like schizophrenia and bipolar disorders, are set around 2.25% of people. In psychiatric hospitals, about 20% of the patients are affected by it. In all outpatient treatments with mental health, BPD affects 10% of those patients. It is a theme to see this disorder around, possibly people you know could have it and no one knew. It seems like a small percentage because only 1 out of 20 people are affected you will still be around that 1. It is best to talk to your doctor if you have concerns beach being undiagnosed will hurt you especially with BPD. You need other's help to get more control of yourself, by treatment or by expressing all of those emotions. You can get past the spot that you are in now. Out professionals tell you that if they are engaged in any type of treatment that they are trying to help better themselves, and that is all they need for a good outcome. You can't figure out everything on your own, you need a new perspective on it. You have been the only one analyzing your brain for all of these years so it will be a change to have another by your side doing the same. They care about you and the outcome you want to also get to. They will listen to whatever you have to say and they could even respond with something that opens a new pathway in your brain, something you have never really thought to do before but now you have heard it just looks so obvious. The benefits outweigh the negatives in this situation because it's worth it to have an improved life. You will start to feel more confident about yourself, you need to feel that self-love. Once you can see the good in you and at the same time control your crisis moments, you will be at peace with yourself.

2

Does Someone You Care About Have BPD

If you know someone with Borderline Personality Disorder than you will have better insight on this next chapter.If someone close to you, a friend or loved one, has BPD then you know it affects you too. If you care about this person then you will need to help them find the proper providers and medications for treatment. You need to be there for them, just in case they have the wrong diagnosis or need assistance. Show lots of support with their decision to stick to the current treatment or to seek better treatment out there.

Your friend could use someone there with emotional support. You need to comfort that inner side of them to help them stay positive. Understand to your hardest what they are going through because it will never be enough in your eyes. Try your hardest to encourage them throughout life. Push them to thrive in every subject they challenge throughout the day.

You have already taken that first step towards helping your friend or relative, just by researching more in-depth about their disorder is enough. You should learn as much as you can about borderline personality disorder and any other mental disorders you can. The more you can learn about the mind and how it can be altered, the closer your loved one will feel to you. If you know why things happen the way they do with BPD then it will be a lot smoother of a ride. If you get written permission from your friend or loved one you can actually talk with his or her therapist to learn about different therapies that involve family members. You can also encourage your loved one with BPD to do family therapies.

One of your biggest responsibilities for caring for your loved one is to make sure that you never ignore any comments about someone with borderline personality disorder intent to harm himself or herself or even someone else. You should report these comments as soon as you hear them to the person's therapist or their doctor. If it is urgent enough and possibly life-threatening then you may need to call the police or just dial 9-1-1.

If you are at all curious about borderline personality disorder or you just want to feel closer to your loved one you should learn more about this. You can go to therapies specifically for significant others and they can teach you the information on it and how you can still be a part of their lives. It is a good idea if you are also wanting to learn about yourself more.

You should be doing something like this if you are married to someone with borderline personality disorder. You can't just act like the problem is not there, it will never go away that way. You married someone that is a challenge, but will be rewarding in due time. You have to put in as much work as they are putting in themselves. You have to be a selfless person who can take a lot, someone who adores helping and is flexible. It is hard to stay together forever with someone who has BPD but it helps when you both are working towards better selves and a better relationship.

Your relationship with your close friend or loved one who has BPD will not change overnight because you went to therapy or because you started to care about the exchange of words more. You have to start building the house before you can decorate it. It will take time, months even years, but for some people, they need this so they can have some stable relationships. I will go into more detail in future chalets on how you can do all of that but I am not at all a therapist who understands and has studied these symptoms for years. Refer to them for further help if you truly want to help rebuild a hurt relationship. You will notice that even after years of you both learning how to treat each other in a relationship that you will have some slips and it all can break loose again. But that happens, no one is perfect. You will always have those emotions and you are just learning on how to tame them inside of you. So, days like those are always going to come and go, you just need to know what thoughts that pass through you should hold on to and the ones you should let in one ear and out the other. You need to know that not every emotion you feel on the inside needs to be brought out in this physical world. It is hard to pinpoint some emotion you are feeling because you feel them and you can't communicate with them.

Reasons like this are why I believe loved ones can help you just as much as your therapist. If you go to a therapist and your family does too, when you aren't around your therapist then that is the time to practice what they preach. Your family is there during those times to help you with what they were taught. They are the personal therapists you get to have for the rest of your day after your session. They can help you and you have to know that is all they want to do so never get upset when they are just trying.

If you are a significant other, loved one, or close friend who knows their friend or loved one has BPD and they aren't doing anything about it you should prepare something to tell them so you can help. They cannot do this on their own because they are stuck in their own minds, they need a therapist to bring them out of the box to see the world as it is. You need to come up to your friend or loved one with the most love and empathy you can have in you, and start the conversation off with ease. You obviously need to research all of this before you go at them for not doing anything positive to help. The best way to bring it up is to keep reassuring them that you love and care about them so much that's why you are doing this.

3 How People Get BPD

Most mental disorders are still being figured out to this day. People are learning new things with the technology we have. Sadly, the cause of some mental disorders, including BPD, aren't completely understood. From what we understand about borderline personality disorder is that it might be caused by environmental factors or genetics. There have been studies shown with twins and with families that the link between BPD and the person with it is their family's history. They could have inherited them from a family member or it could be very strongly associated with any other mental disorder that they are diagnosed with. Other research has shown that the people that carry BPD also could have some brain abnormalities. Studies have been done and they can see the changes in aggression, impulsiveness, and regulating your emotions. Also, in function with that, certain brain chemicals may not function as well as others. Mostly the chemical is serotonin.

There are a few risk factors for people to be a predisposition for this disorder. The way your personality develops can be a fraction of the reason why you are the way you are. There is always going to be hereditary links within your family. If your close relative has this disorder or a similar linked disorder, you could be prone to it at birth. That isn't always the case though, there have been many people with borderline personality disorder that report they have been sexually or physically abused even neglected during childhood. Those years are your most important years, they are the building blocks to the beginning of your life. You can also have had some experiences being lost and/or separated from your guardian. That pulls you closer to the abandonment that you will always feel even when it's not there. Every incident in your life has changed you into you. Even just watching and experiencing your guardian do heavy substance abuse, especially if they have a mental disorder of their own. Family relationships affect you so much when you are growing up, the more native the more negative down the line you will feel about life.

Any hostile or just unstable ties in your family are not good to have. As a child, you don't really understand what is right and wrong when your parents do things because you assume that they are the all-knowing parents. You think whatever your parents are doing to you is what is happening to everyone around the world, you think of your reception as everyone's perception. That's why at this age you need to be in a healthy and stable household. If you are genetically inclined to BPD then you should have your family be your support, not your punching bag.

Even your own personality traits that you have built upon yourself can affect your mental state. Some personality traits linked to borderline personality disorder are anger, aggression, and impulsivity. In your mind, you have a garden, a garden of all your emotions. The emotions you feed and water the most will grow the tallest, the ones you give into start to take over. You need to learn how to evenly spread out your water because you

15

can't let your anger and aggressiveness be the pilot of your life. You can fly the plane pretty well by yourself.

If you are an outsider wanting to learn more about this disorder and how you can help a loved one then you can also see the signs of when they are falling off the rails. Usually, you know when the BPD has taken over but you truly need to see the full circle of why they are the way that they are. If you see your loved one constantly changing their job or just being fired, you should talk to them. Let them know how great you see them, and how they aren't alone. If they don't complete their education or just drop out, see why. You can always push them to do things that they probably didn't think they could accomplish or it could just be a nice conversation about why they didn't like the schooling there were getting. If they are getting into constant legal issues, especially jail time, then talking to them will help get feeling off their chest that they probably didn't say out of their head until that moment. If your relationship with them is straining or you see their personal relationship filled with constant conflict then you can always step in to help. If it's not your relationship, then don't give any tips and tricks for their significant other. Just tell them that they can do so much to help their relationship with therapies made for spouses of BPD patients or taking time to learn about themselves. You don't want to interject into someone's relationship but you can always help push them into making their own decisions that will help them in the end.

If it is your relationship then just do everything I said up there for yourself. You can take some time out and figure out you and why you both work together. Having therapy helps too, you can do family therapy with your whole family so you all can be comfortable with talking to each other emotionally, or you can do single therapy with a therapist who specializes in BPD loved ones. It's becoming a more common theme to have more therapies for this because it's becoming more of a widespread issue. You should always help them and see the person inside is trying. It's much harder for people with BPD to not just put emotion into everything they say. Some people with BPD can also be associated with another mental illness so you always need to know that anything can happen with them and that this is more of a struggle for them than it is for you. So, I know you can get through it.

The most common mental disorders to have in correlation with borderline personality disorder are alcohol or any other substance abuse, anxiety disorders, attention deficit or hyperactivity disorders, bipolar disorders, depression, eating disorders, and post-traumatic stress disorder.

4

How to Feel Empowered and Boost Your Confidence While Having BPD

It is very hard for people to boost up their self-esteem, but it is a million times harder for people with BPD. Self-esteem is the way we think about ourselves. If you have BPD, you could possibly have very low self-esteem and that can have a negative impact on your life. The stronger your self-esteem is the more time you can remain confident, strong, and easily connect with other people. If you have borderline personality disorder then feeling good about yourself is very rare, instead, you might feel underutilized or worthless more often. There are easy ways to build yourself up and be confident in the person you have blossomed into.

With BPD, you might be only able to assert your feeling and thoughts through anger. You need to learn how to work past that and express yourself calmly. You need to express how you are feeling without personal attack. It will take some time before your subconscious starts to understand this as well but by then I'm hoping communication will be a breeze.

It might help you see the good in yourself if you remember the good that people have seen in you in the past. Try to keep a little journal and write down every compliment that someone gives you. In the moment of writing it down you will get a great feeling and on your worst of days, that is a wonderful book to help brighten your mood.

You really need to focus on your positive qualities. You need to remember that every single person has those awful qualities that aren't as desirable but your overall goodness inside of you will always outweigh your negatives. You might only be able to name a couple positives on the top of your head but if you wanted to you can use that same journal and compile a list of everything you enjoy in yourself. I swear to you that list will just keep growing and growing the more you think. You truly are a gift to this world and seeing that in yourself is like heaven.

If you get those little voices in your head telling you how awful you are doing or that you are going to mess up then you should talk back to those voices and tell them they've got it all wrong. This is the one time in your life you need to talk back because those mental preparations before anything can change the entire outcome. Be positive in yourself and I swear it will all turn out positive in the end. How you treat and talk to yourself can make a huge difference in the outcome of any situation.

You need to also open up your eyes to the rest of the world because they are all worried about the same image you are putting up for yourself. Everyone is trying to learn that self-love and is thinking that everyone is talking about them. Ease up a little bit, we are all too into ourselves to be judging and talking about others. Just focus on yourself and you will see yourself growing. If by now you truly wanted that journal then here is another thing to write down in it; every evening, just write down all your accomplishments for the day. Everything you did that made you proud to be you or even just things you handled well. It doesn't have to be big, it could be just to remember to brush your teeth in the morning. Your brain makes notes of your successes and it encourages you to move towards those goals.

When it comes time to be confident, you may find yourself in your head, going over all of the worst-case scenarios that may come along with attempting to do whatever it is you are trying to do. It is important to keep in mind is that the only way you will ever be more confident is if you take the first step. If you find yourself still having trouble then the following tips might be useful.

Try and reframe your anxiety, if you are unsure about what the outcome of a certain event is going to be, that uncertainty can manifest itself as anticipation which can easily become fear with the right triggers. If you react in a situation where you would benefit from being self-confident with anxiety, you will lose the momentum you might have had going in the situation. Instead, you may find it helpful to react to anxiety as if it were curiosity instead. Rather than being anxious about what's to come, trick your mind into being curious about what is going to happen instead. If you can think of the experience as a type of experiment, you will gain a level of detachment from the situation that will make it much easier for you to power through in the long run. Curiosity and self-confidence go together much more easily than anxiety and self-confidence and you may find that curiously helps your confident momentum continue.

If that doesn't work, you might find success instead in taking the time to consider why it is that you are really afraid. If you find you always respond to similar instances that require self-confidence in a negative way you might need to take a look inside and consider why this is the case. It could be because your mind is finding patterns where no true pattern exists which may mean you are responding to stimuli as you perceive them, not the way the situation is actually presenting itself.

To combat this, the next time you start to feel nervous or scare before having to be self-confident, simply take an extra moment to consider the situation as it truly is and consider what it is about the scenario that is making you feel the way you do. If nothing specific comes to mind then odds are you are about to act based on false information, no matter how real it may have seemed at the time.

When you are just getting the hang of being more self-confident, you will likely experience moments where your mind throws up apparent roadblocks to your success. The most typical version of this involves some type of worst-case scenario that may occur if you take a predetermined course of action. While these scenarios are likely going to be extremely convincing in the moment, they are likely only going to be based on the dimmest version of reality and are likely going to have little bearing on what will actually happen which is why it is generally going to be better to just push forward with what you were planning to do and ignore them.

While may well be easier said than done, focusing on the fact that everyone has their own issues to deal with can make failing much easier to handle. All you need to do is tell yourself that what might seem like the end of the world to you, is likely just everyone else's Tuesday. While it may be hard, try to keep in mind that failure alone is nothing to be ashamed of, and trying and failing once will likely make the second time much more manageable.

Consider what there is to learn from the current situation, even if you fail. If you stop focusing on how you are going to be embarrassed if you fail, you may realize that there wasn't that much to worry about, to begin with. Without the added pressure, you may even find that you succeed. What's more, if you stop focusing on the failure and start focusing on whatever it is you are doing and maybe actually learn from your mistakes.

When trying to find the nerve to do something you have never done before, you may find that it helps if you just consider the odds. It's like the lottery says, you can't win if you never play. If rather than running every time an opportunity to show self-confidence shows up, you instead make an effort to take full advantage of the situation you will find that over time, you will succeed at least as often as you fail. What's more, you will find that slowly but surely being self-confident may actually become a habit.

What you really just need to do is stop thinking about all the ways that you are going to try and be more self-confident in the future, and instead start focusing on how you can improve your interactions with others in the present. Remember, all the good intentions in the world won't amount to much of anything if you don't put them into practice once in a while. While stretching out of your comfort zone will naturally be difficult at first, the fact that it is just as difficult for everyone else should do something to bring you a little comfort. Don't forget, the only difference between you and the people you admire for their self-confidence is that they had the determination to take the first step towards self-improvement.

If, after considering these tips and suggestions you just don't see yourself being a pillar of self-confidence, then you may be better off just faking it. While this might seem like a joke, you will be surprised at how effective faking confidence can actually be. For example, imagine an interaction with the most confident person you know. Now, imagine that same conversation except the other person was faking their level of self-confidence the entire time. It's a fact that the only difference between a conversation where you appear to have self-confidence, and a conversation where you actually have self-confidence is how you end up feeling on the inside. If you still aren't convinced, go ahead and try it once, you are sure to be surprised by the results. What's more, if you continue pretending long enough, eventually the act will be indistinguishable from reality, even to you. Until you get to that point, however, you may want to keep some of the following tips in mind.

First things first, think back to the person you thought of as the pinnacle of self-confidence in the previous example, when you are still learning to respond to things in the way that a self-confident person would, all you need to do is ask yourself what that person would do in whatever situation you happen to find yourself in. Don't be vague when you ask this question either, the more specific you can get the better. Consider the way the confident person moves, how they respond in conversation, the way they use their body language to really get their point across and what their speech patterns are like and then do everything in your power to act the same way.

One of the most important facets of appearing self-confident is changing the way you walk and stand. If you have self-confidence then you are going to naturally be more inclined to stand up straight with your shoulders squared. Those with low self-confidence, on the other hand, are more likely to slouch and slump when they talk. To project a more self-confident image, then, all you need to do is make a point of assuming the correct posture whenever talking to others, don't forget to always look them in the eye as well. Those with high levels of self-confidence also always walk as if they have someplace that they need to be because they are important and so is their time. If you want to look more confident than you feel, simply adopting a walking speed that is about a fourth faster than average should start to make a noticeable difference on the way others perceive you.

If you think back to your self-confidence idol, you will likely realize that they tend to pay a lot of compliments to others. This is because they often feel so good about themselves that they can't help but share the love with those around them. As such, making a point of complimenting others more will naturally cause them to assume you are more self-confident that you really are. What's more, starting off a conversation with a compliment is a great way to naturally segue into an additional small talk. It is also important that you consider the version of yourself that you are presenting to the world. When someone is self-confident, other people tend to see them as outgoing, friendly and happy. Thus, you can reverse engineer the same results by making it a point to be all three to those you meet on a regular basis.

For starters, you are going to want to always introduce yourself to others before they have the chance to do the same, and also smiling more. Introducing yourself tells the other person that you have self-respect and thus you deserve their respect as well. Furthermore, you are going to want to fully commit yourself to any group activities that you find yourself a part of, and don't shy away from participating in group discussion as well. When you do speak, make it a point to avoid filler words such as like or um, words like these make it seem as though you aren't sure what you are going to say next or that you are uncertain of the point you are trying to make. Taken as a whole, these activities will naturally make you seem like someone who is more self-confident.

How to Cope with BPD with 5 STEPS to Balanced Responses

Now, this is a simple coping technique that has been a positive way to help people with a form of Cognitive Behavior Therapy. You have to know that if you want these steps to help you have to do more than just knowing them, you have to apply them. Changes won't happen overnight but if you keep at it and it becomes a normal thing for you then it can do wonders. I have confidence that if anyone puts their mind to it and actually uses it practically every day, they can change. But that will take every day having patience, giving time, and just practicing.

You will not master this right away so don't give up. I know it will be challenging but don't expect to master them right away. If you don't do so good one day then all you need to do is get back up on that horse and ride one, try harder next time and I know it will go better. Even if you aren't at the stage you want to be yet, it will be better than the last. Once you work these steps into your hindsight or even retrospectively will help you, but I can say even if you practice this for years or even practice this for decades you can be halted by your pie under desires. You have to remember all of the years of your old behaviors you are trying to change, it is going to be a process.

First, whenever you are feeling your feelings coming in you need to stop in your place. Just breathe for a second and try to analyze your feelings. Is it because you are angry? Maybe you are angry over a certain situation. Could you be feeling lonely at the moment? Maybe you are possibly just tired and needing a break from everything to sleep. You need to analyze yourself and see what you are feeling. You need to remember that whatever you are feeling is very physical and will always be temporary. Always remember that whatever you are feeling is in that moment. You don't always have to give in to every emotion, once you realize that in a day or two that this feeling on the inside is temporary you will be glad you kept it in instead letting it out all over your closest relationships.

Second, just figure out what the problem is. Figure out why you are feeling the way that you are feeling and what might have caused it. You might even come up with more than one problem at the moment, but whatever you find is annoying you should be written down on a piece of paper. Once you can centralize the problem you can start working past it or overcoming it. It becomes easier once you start figuring out your r own thoughts and why they come and go. The problem might not be super clear, you could just be filled with emotions and that's okay. Just don't feed into those emotions when you should remember that they are only temporary.

Third, you need to focus on your problems and try to work past them. The best way is when you write down every problem you should come up with three different solutions on how to fix it. You don't need ten and you can't have just one. You need choice in your life, and when every choice is given by yourself it makes it easier to make a decision. Every path in life always separates into smaller paths so you should know that every decision isn't going to be a straightforward solution. Some solutions work for some and not for others, that is why you need to be in control of your own self. I know you can do it because once you do I swear it feels like your high in the clouds.

Fourth, you should take some time to go over those options and make a choice. This choice doesn't have to be permanent, you can always try going a new route. If you pick something and go for it then you are the god of your own universe. If it doesn't end up working the way you thought it would, then don't get emotional at all. You can always rework the system and follow the steps again and try a new path. Even trying the other two ideas if you wanted would help you get down the path.

Fifth, you honestly just need to do it all! If you are reading this then that means you are still on this planet, it means you have survived with yourself for this long so you can go so much further. Nothing will change your own problem or issue you are experiencing until you do something about it. It doesn't have to fix the problem completely, even small acts towards yourself will help you. You can't go forward or backward until you start moving so just believe in yourself and try hard to go forward. To change your perspective or outlook on a situation you would have to change a little part of your inner self. You need to have that change be set in stone for when you want the outside world to see it because that is the only way to change the effect on how they see you is to keep it for a long time. You can't try for a day because people won't see the change in you, they can't tell the difference in that short amount of time.

If you are wanting to try these steps to help yourself get ahead in life, then first try with an old problem that has been bugging you. Maybe even a recent situation that has happened. You want to practice on this not spur of the moment so you know how to use these to your advantage. Always be checking your halt, your first step to having a balanced response. If you can check in with your emotions and actually understand them, then you can escalate to a positive point in your life. Once your conscious and subconscious kick in and realize there are better ways to deal with all of these stressful situations, you can apply the full five-step approach with ease. Everything in life that's good takes time, I truly believe you have it in you to give yourself this time. In a few years, you would be happy that you can analyze your situations and not just explode all over everyone that comes near you.

6 How to Accept Yourself and Add on Positive Effects

The first thing you have to understand is that no one hates you as much as you hate yourself. You need to ease up and relax about yourself, find the parts you enjoy and help them grow. I understand that people don't want to express themselves because they are always worried that others will judge them if they knew who they really were. But you have to realize that people won't reject you, and the ones that do are horrible people so you don't need them in your life.

There are pure people and people who take advantage, you need to be around those pure people because they will show you a new side of yourself. You can raise your confidence and no be scared of rejection. The only thing you would need to apply is the self-realization of your emotions. You need to be aware and hold back when you can. You can grow positive relationships this way and people could actually love you for just the person you always are.

Self-acceptance can be a magical thing when you have a borderline personality disorder because it allows you to feel that love and see it while right infant of the face of abandonment. You will learn to love others with their own flaws like they have learned to love yours. You can see the world is all so internally focused on their cracks in their personality that you aren't different at all. You will start to love yourself in the healthiest of ways and be more positive about yourself. It takes away that need to find acceptance through doing risky behavior. It helps you when those suicidal thoughts come and you can just shut them down. It helps you realize when your moods aren't stable and you need to find the balance. It also shows you when your mood is balled and you can see the serine pleasure of the calmness.

When you become unstable your more aware of the feeling, it doesn't just open the floodgates. You will finally feel like a whole person, someone who can fulfill their dreams. You will see yourself getting angry less of the time and it will become more of an uncommon thought that flows through your mind. You won't have to live afraid anymore, you can be yourself and be confident in who you are. The more confident you are the more people will come, and they hopefully will be positive experiences in your life instead of past negative relationships.

To see all of your good, you have to focus on your strengths inside. You can feed those to be stronger and while you are doing them, you can feed your insecurities. Everyone has them so you should be proud of what you have, the more open you are to others about yourself internally, but in a positive way, the better people will understand what you are going through. You don't have to feel so alone all of the time. There are people in the world who just like to help. There are people who always will speak negatively towards you and they are the people who just like to hurt you or push you down.

You don't need to deal with those types of people forever, the sooner you cut off every toxic relationship the better you will feel. If you can cut them off then you should try to fix it by learning more about yourself or going to couple's therapy. You can always fix relationships but some cannot be repaired because the people on the other side are not willing to change their awful ways. You need to find those people who make you feel great and create a support system out of them. You can't just lean one person, so having system would be ideal. The people that are accepting of who you are no matter what you have done and believe you can still go up from here are the ones you need.

Take to them first before you mentally put them in a category of people you can fall back on. Some can't take the responsibility or they kindly don't want to, that is okay because they are still a friend you can talk to when you are hanging out with them. You should have a few people that when something happens you can just call them or see them so you don't have a meltdown. People who like doing this for you exist, so get out of your negative canon and find these people.

The more negativity you surround yourself in the more you are going to feel suffocated. You shouldn't beat yourself up for anything in the past. If you can't even forgive yourself then why would you assume that others would do it for you? You will always have regrets but if all you are doing is examining those regrets you will never be able to practice your acceptance. You should forgive yourself as soon as it happens and move on. You shouldn't just forget about it though, you need to learn from it. That is how you grow as a human.

We all have tons of flaws and if we looked back in every bad decision we made then we would never go forward as a human race. You made your best decision with the information you had up available to you at the time. You can't beat yourself up about it because it's a memory. You are going to miss out on the greatness of the now if you are always focusing on the past.

A reason why you might beat yourself up all the time is the inner critic you have inside. It's the voice that is always showing you the insecurities and judgment. Some think of this voice as their internal voice of reason, so they are always listening to it. Do not feed into your internal harsh critic that we all have. You can start to quiet that voice by calming down and telling it that I am only human, I am doing all I can do. Failures are opportunities for a new way of learning and growth. Always speak to the highest version of yourself, the best version of you. That is who you want to talk to because the more you converse with it the more it will be brought out into your external image.

7

Awareness of Crisis Situations

It is very hard to open your mind if you don't have BPD to a crisis situation because you have never experienced it. Those moments of pure happiness or furious anger are your strongest moments, for someone with borderline personality disorder those emotions are like their normal day to day emotions. Crisis attacks are about ten times as intense as those normal emotions. It is hard to control, especially the farther you get into the crisis. You can always prevent it from happening if you think about your words before you say them. You should analyze all that you say and then you can say it, you don't have to be bluntly negative all the time.

To start to be aware of your crisis you might get a chemical change inside your body, that could be making you shake or making you irrational. That is your body getting ready for the crisis and expressing itself before you let it out. You will also get all of this anger and these thoughts flowing into your mind, your goal is to not catch a single one. You should let them go in one ear and out the other. Don't feed the bear, just be nice and polite with your conversations. What you give out to people is hopefully what you revive back from them, and the more positive it all is the more the positivity flows through you. If you can't hold back then just try to distract yourself with something, it could be reading your favorite book, watching a comedy, or even just going straight to the computer and typing out all of your feelings onto all of those pages. It just helps ease your feelings inside and help you get back to your normal levels. Anything you can do to go back to your normal levels is a good idea because the more you practice getting to that point the more easy and painless it will be to get there. Just believe in yourself, and that you can do it. If you need an extra push with support or therapy then take it because I know you can always be a better you. We all can. The effort you put in is the effort that comes back, so if you try to get better and stick to it for months or years and put in effort, you will see a return. You will always feel these symptoms during a crisis situation but over time they can get smaller and smaller, easier and easier to handle. Time is the key intros one, and the lock will take a lot of patience.

If you are in a crisis situation and none of your security web is there to talk to then there are still other options for you so you don't have to have an emotional event. 1-800-SUICIDE is always available to talk to you if you get to that dire state of your mind. They can be reached 24 hours a day

37

because they genuinely care about people like you. They want to be there for you so nothing happens to you. You are very special and you don't realize it sometimes, especially when you are younger. There is also the Alcohol and Drug Information and Referral Service, which is if you are having a negative induced by that. It is available to anyone and you can call this number if you are concerned about a loved one with abuse. The number is 604-660-9382 and they are available like the suicide line all 24 hours of the day. The people on the other side of the phone genuinely want to hear what is upsetting you and how they can help you move past it. One more number you can call is 811, they are there for anything. You can call for any nonemergency health information, that includes all mental health information. You can also call this number to speak to a registered nurse if you are worried about any symptoms you have. If you have medicine questions then you can talk to a pharmacist as well.

There are many paths to take when you are in the moment, but you need to train yourself over time which paths are good to go down and which ones you should try to avoid. You are in control of everything you say and so you can make the situation less anger filled and more pleasure filled. You want to come out with a problem but do it in an approachable way that isn't harsh or demanding. You can practice how to do this in your free time with past reasons you got mad and how you could have handled it better. You are going to practice a lot because this won't just come naturally to you. But I believe you can do anything you set your mind to. Just watch out because you might have some anger slips at the beginning of your training, but after a few months, you will start to get in this new groove. It will be a very, very hard goal to get to but it will help take a strain off of your relationships, your job, your everyday life, and so much more. The sooner you start to apply this the sooner you will get results. I believe that any person at any age can do this, but it will get harder the older you get. When you start this change, you have to remember that you have been in this awful mindset your whole life.

You have to change your old habits and it will take years and years to cover these habits. Once you can control your emotions and your inner love towards yourself you will feel like a new man. Don't expect all of your symptoms to ever go away, you will always have them but at the end of your training, they will be reduced immensely. You will not be triggered as fast or as often.

Additionally, you will likely feel better if you institute a safety plan that you can rely on when you find yourself in the midst of suicidal thoughts or another type of high-risk behavior. Without this type of plan, you may end up in a situation where you are in danger of hurting yourself or someone else. Having a plan in place in case everything goes wrong will make it more difficult for you to take an action in the heat of the moment that you will possibly regret for the rest of your life. Additionally, it is important to keep in mind that the plan creation tips below can only be utilized properly when you or a loved one are in full control of their cognitive facilities, not when they are in the midst of serious crisis.

The first thing you are going to need to do is to talk to a professional about the ideas you have for your safety plan. Depending on your specific situation, they may recommend several different things, such as including or removing specific aspects based on your personalized needs. If you do not currently have someone who can work on a safety plan with you, it is important that you find a professional to talk with right away. If it is the stigma of seeing a therapist that is keeping you away, it is important to persevere, therapy was literally created for people in your situation.

Once you have spoken to a therapist, you will need their help when it comes to evaluating your potential dangers and risks including things such as suicidal thoughts, urges of violence, or thoughts of harming others no matter how fleeting they may be. Issues such as these are all going to be the primary target of your safety plan so it is crucial that you sit down and take the time to think things through before you discuss your issues with your therapist so that your ultimate plans end up working out as fully as possible.

In addition to helping you evaluate your current risk level, it is also important to keep in mind various factors in your life that may be escalating any of those potential dangers such as improper medication use or unhealthy relationships. If you own a weapon and depending on your situation, your healthcare provider may recommend turning the weapon over to the authorities for everyone's safety.

Once you know what the symptoms and behaviors you need to deal with are, you will be ready to start looking for their sources by identifying triggers. As an example, it is common for those who suffer from BPD to have issues dealing with abandonment which can lead to either real or imagined slight in this regard to be extremely troubling to deal with. If you understand that you have issues in this regard you can then be more aware of your triggers and what you can do in order to ensure they crop up as infrequently as possible.

In order to determine your triggers, the first thing you are going to want to do is to find a private place to record your thoughts. It is important to be aware that this exercise could potentially cause you distress, simply because you will be thinking about a lot of specific situations that are tied directly to your symptoms so you are going to want to be in a private place where you can plan for some soothing afterward.

Take a piece of paper and draw three columns on it. The first should be labeled trigger, the second emotion and the third response to emotion. You will then want to take some time and consider the last time you experienced an extremely negative emotional response. This could be something like emptiness, shame, sadness, fear, loneliness or anger. In the trigger column, you will want to write down the event that triggers the emotional response you remember, being as specific and detailed as you need to be. Remember, the goal here is to catalog issues to be avoided in the future so the more specific you can be about your triggers the better.

Additionally, when you are searching your memory for triggers, keep in mind that this could be either something internal or something external. It could be something obvious such as a fight you had with a loved one or it could simply be a depressing stray thought. When listing your triggers, it is important to examine the situation that spawned the response from every angle, it is possible that what you first consider the obvious trigger could actually be an ancillary part of the story. Find the true root triggers of your emotions for the best success.

Perhaps the most common triggers for BPD have something to do with interpersonal relationships. It is common for those with BPD to experience thoughts of suicide, self-harm, anger, fear or other impulsive behavior after situations occur that lead to them feeling either abandoned, criticized or rejected. For example, it is likely that when you call a friend and they don't call you back you will likely have a series of spiraling thoughts about why your friend no longer likes you, why they are not calling you back and what it means for your friendship. This, in turn, leads to feelings of anger, sadness or an urge for self-harm.

Some individuals with BPD experience triggers that come in the form thoughts that appear as if from nowhere. This is especially true for those who experienced extreme forms of trauma when they were younger as intense emotions related to feelings from those times can often trigger the symptoms of BPD. This memory doesn't necessarily need to be all that distressing in and of itself either, happy memories can also lead to feelings that things are not as good now as they once were which can cause a spiral into depression.

When it comes to the emotion column you are going to want to fill in the emotional response you had to the trigger in question. It is important to not limit yourself to a single emotion per trigger as it is perfectly natural to feel multiple things once a trigger occurs. However, it is important to not force an emotional label on a specific trigger, if you can't determine exactly what you felt in the moment, it is better to leave the space blank than to incorrectly categorize the trigger. With this in mind, it is also important that you don't avoid listing emotions because you don't want to deal with the consequences of doing so, the purpose of the exercise is to improve in the long run after all, which makes the difficulty more than worth it.

In the final column, you are going to write down the way you responded to the feelings that the trigger caused. As an example, if you felt extremely ashamed because of a specific trigger then the action may be self-harm. The situations you list don't all have to be negative, however, as there is a benefit to being able to see, written out in front of you, the things you did right as well. For example, you could have gotten angry after a specific trigger but perhaps you used coping skills as a means of managing that anger effectively. Once you have successfully determined your list of triggers, you may find it helpful to revisit your list on a regular basis, if only to see how far you have come.

With the list in front of you, you are going to want to look at the triggers column and determine if you can see any patterns developing there. In general, most people will be able to determine a few different primary categories that their triggers are grouped around. One common grouping of triggers for people with BPD is a perceived sense of rejection. While eventually, you will discover most if not all of your triggers, during the early days you are going to want to keep it with you and add to it every time something list-worthy happens throughout your day. Keeping the list on you will also make you more aware of moments where your triggers have come into play, hopefully making it easier for you to resist giving into the negative response in time.

Once you are aware of your triggers, you will be able to get to work on avoiding them, some of which are going to be easier to avoid than others. Likewise, some triggers will be impossible to avoid, while still others will be better for you to deal with face to face. Overall, avoidance is a strategy that should be used as sparingly as possible. It is better to make coping with issues part of your plan as opposed to simply avoiding them as you will then have no plan in place for when the avoidance plan fails.

Instead, a good option is to approach scenarios where you feel you will have to come face to face with your triggers in a strategic fashion. While productive, this method can be stressful and it is recommended that you proceed with the help of a therapist. When you are first getting started it is best to work with a small trigger so that you can face it in a controlled and limited way.

As an example, if you find that the idea of failure is one of your biggest triggers, then you can face it in a small way first, such as by trying a yoga pose that you know you are unable to do. Make a point of trying this pose regularly, and then when you fail you can be aware of the various physical and emotional responses you are feeling so you can start dealing with them in a more positive way. Rather than feeling disappointed or rejected, you may find that you can cope in a more positive way possible through meditation or maybe even just by laughing at yourself. The specifics don't matter, all that really does is that you learn to face the idea of failing without resorting to behavior that is destructive to yourself or others.

If you feel as though your triggers typically send you into an emotional loop you can't seem to break free from, try writing down a handful of things you can do to manage your emotions and break yourself out of the cycle the next time you experience a trigger. You can then keep this list on you at all times, you will be surprised at how just having the list on you can help prevent you from ending up in a destructive loop. When the trigger does occur, don't hesitate, pull out the list and try what you have written down, if the first one doesn't work then go onto the next and then the next. Go through the whole list, multiple times if needed, whatever you need to free yourself from the loop. Knowing you have an out when it comes to a particularly aggressive trigger will often go a long way towards making it feel more manageable which will often prevent it from triggering anything at all.

When working on your safety plan, you are going to primarily want to focus on the triggers that have the biggest potential of leading you to harm yourself or others as the goal should be to keep you as safe as possible. You can think of these as resources to help you cope that you can use before your symptoms get so severe that you end up in a full-blown mental health crisis.

Now that your plan is coming together you are going to want to commit it to paper. You should have a list of your riskiest behaviors, their triggers, plans for coping when things get out of hand along with ways to respond in case you find yourself in an emergency scenario. You will then want to put all of these together to ensure that you have a reliable, step by step plan of action ready to go in case you really need it. While it is a lot of work up front, as soon as you use it for the first time you will realize just how worth it all the effort was.

With each behavior, you are going to want to write out the issues that trigger it, several useful coping responses that can get you out of the mental loop the trigger causes, what to do if they don't work and how to avoid an impending emergency situation. Once you have a list of all the risks you need to keep in mind, and how you will deal with them, the last thing you will need to do is to make a promise to yourself to stick to your safety plan as much as possible, and mean it. Making a conscious choice, when you are in a reliable mental state will make it easier to not think and just follow the outlined steps when you need them the most. Waiting to commit can lead to situations where you lose your resolve in the moment, which can shove all the hard work and planning you did down the drain. Depending on your personal situation, your therapist might even recommend having you sign the plan.

8

Cutting Edge Treatments and Cures

People with BPD need to find a way to just cope with how they are internally. It helps having someone there to guide them along. The main treatment that is provided for people with borderline personality disorder is using psychotherapy. Some can have medication as well or even hospitalization with the therapy. Treating your disorder instead of just ignoring it can make you feel so much more positive towards yourself and just live a more structured life, it gets rewarding once you have given it the time it needs. You can't expect overnight changes, you are going to have to put in the effort to become a more stable you.

The first path that you can take with BPD is doing psychotherapy. It has another name of talk therapy and is a very common treatment towards borderline personality disorder. Your therapist will then be comfortable with your BPD and already be acquainted with the disorder. They can also shape your therapy around your own personal needs and growths. Psychotherapists only are there to help you, they understand what you are going through and hey will come towards you with the least aggressive perception of your reality. They will help if you let them in and give effort back.

Psychotherapists are there to meet the needs you are wanting to achieve, they will do a lot to help. They are analyzing your ability to function in the moment and see how much it can improve. Also, you will be at least slightly able to control your own emotions, especially taking comfortably to an unknown person. They are there to focus on your feelings with you and analyze them so you can reduce your impulsivity and control your actions from the feelings. You should also learn how to bring up your relationships to a nice level by being completely aware of how you are expressing your emotions and how they are doing the same. Obviously, they will overall just inform you about borderline personality disorder. You might know a lot about it but they will fill in those cracks that will help keep your human structure together. It is worth having a second perspective on your life when you know that they are only there to help. They won't leave you until you are on the right track and they will be supportive just like you have needed for your whole life.

If you are in any way curious of psychotherapy then you could research the subcategories of the therapy. There will always be new technologies available and new treatments out there so here are six different therapies that I can suggest. First, you could take Dialectical behavior therapy in a group setting or individual setting. This therapy is specifically targeted towards people with borderline personality disorder. It is more based on skills to teach you in a comfortable way. It teaches you how to maintain your emotions, deal with internal stress, and improve the quality of every relationship.

Another way you can be treated is with Schema-Focused therapy. As like Dialectical behavior therapy, you can talk this in a group setting or you can do it in an in-divide setting. It will help you face your unmet needs and desires deep down that have led you down the path you have taken. It could have caused bad patterns in life that can be a problem when you are an adult. Those experiences can hurt many parts of your life and daily life. This therapy mainly focuses on your life path and helping you walk down it in a brighter light. All that they want to see is you starting a life pattern that is just completely positive. The third choice would be Metallization-based therapy, which is a type of talk therapy. It helps you to express yourself any unknown or known internal thoughts and feelings. It helps you create a different perspective on your situation but still through your own eyes. You will understand why you are feeling the way you are from seeing it in a whole new way.

Mentalization-based therapy is going to be all about thinking before you apply the action. There is also the System training for emotional

50

predictability and problem-solving, STEPPS is the acronym. It is a treatment that you would have to dedicate yourself to, it is a process. It takes 20 weeks to complete and you work in a group setting. You are in groups that are with your loved ones, caregivers, close friends, or spouses. This psychotherapy is used in correlation to any other of these therapies. It helps them apply what they are learning as they are learning it. It also helps your close family and friends to see what you are actually going through.

Next, we have Transference-focused psychotherapy which is also called psychodynamic psychotherapy. It is there to help you understand your emotions and internal struggles with a one on one connection you grow with your therapist. They will help mold your brain to open your eyes to all sides of you. They want to help you get on the right path so you should apply everything you hear in your therapy sessions out in your real life. Lastly, there is General psychiatric management. This therapy is about finding yourself internally and passing all the conflicts as well as dealing with your outer emotions. It is a common therapy and it is usually conjoined with medicine, group therapies, family education on BPD, and more individual therapies.

If you are wanting to make the path of medicine, then there is some good and bad. There is the medicine that can help, but not completely. There have been no drugs approved yet by the FDA that is specifically used as a treatment for borderline personality disorder. There are certain medications out there that can help with your symptoms or reoccurring problems like anxiety, aggression, depression, and impulsivity.

These medications could be in the classes of antidepressants, antipsychotics, or even just mood stabilizing drugs. The one person who will definitely know what is best for you to take is your primary care provider. They will know what symptoms you needed relieved and they could give you the best option, or even if they think medicine is a good option. There will be side effects from some so you should have caution if you are curious about this step.

In a small chance that you need a firmer treatment than therapy, you can go to a hospital or clinic that specializes in psychiatric help. This can be a positive place to be especially if you have had thoughts or actions of self-inflicted injury or suicide. You will be under care for a long time there, not just an appointment. It is a hard step for some people to take but others really need this push to start seeing themselves in a different light.

Always remember that learning all of these treatments of expressing and understanding your inner self and external words will never happen easy. You are going have to work for it, but if you have come this far in life then I know you can handle this challenge. It takes a long time to reverse how you have been living for all of this time. Be patient because it will come. Your thoughts and behaviors will take time until they become a subconscious act to be positive. You might have to wait months or even years to see the outcome and stick with therapy the whole ride. You won't ever get completely cured, you will just learn how to deal with it better and control it. Years after, you could still struggle with a few of your symptoms but just give it time. You will always go through waves of your symptoms coming and going, control those emotions and you can feel better about yourself.

9

Building Relationships

People who experience borderline personality disorder have a hard time developing relationships and keeping them stable. It is hard to get personally connected with others with the way they express their emotions. But it is very hard for people with BPD to be alone, they are stuck in their head and stuck thinking about abandonment issues. All of that just keeps adding to the anxiety. People with BPD have a hard time easing their anger and also like to undermine their spouse. You can barely see this process because people like to mask their dependence towards someone and manipulation. They have an unstable view of their own self, which leads to impulse decisions and very demanding confrontations.

It's a sad cycle of love and relationships for people with BPD. But don't think this of all relationships, some can get passed this cycle People with BPD usually abuse something like substances and it creates conflict. You are wanting that connection but still fighting with them like a child. Most partners will have this conflict and if they cannot work past it can come to divorce and even domestic violence. Reasons like these with relationships is why people with BPD have a very hard time giving their trust to others.

You need people around your life that are like a sponge to your emotions and won't break from what you say. It is very common to have wrongful anger and many breakdowns with the people that are close in your life. It's not because you don't care for them, it's actually the opposite. Most symptoms of borderline personality disorder are equivalent to love addiction. Now, this isn't an actual diagnosis but you can see it within people with addictive behavior. You can see this in others by how past their relationships grow and how passionate it is right out of the gate.

People with BPD cannot see the issues in their partner and don't have a very open mind to intimacy changes. No matter how great your partner is, they will disappoint you in one way or another because they will always conceive it in their black and white thought pattern. It might not have been put off in the way you received it. You need to learn how to responsibly deal with your emotions, especially towards the ones you love.

There was a study done that showed people with borderline personality disorder showing they actually have a different sense of every social norm, so it impacts their mind and ability to give trust or listen while cooperating. When a relationship has something go wrong, people with BPD do not respond in a way to fix the issue. That causes the significant other to not want to fully cooperate with him in the future. People with BPD can hardly get passed their own emotional screen to look at what others are going through.

They are so opus on themselves because just seeing their emotions and dealing with them is a huge hurdle. Especially in women, research shows that people experiencing borderline personality disorder have problems with sexual attitude and patterns of very unstable relationships. They use sexuality as a way to avoid the emptiness experienced inside and helps with tampering your anxiety you have felt during previous abandonment.

People experiencing BPD do not think in the way that they are ever satisfied emotionally. They can definitely still give out their needs emotionally in a positive healthy way. But, as soon as they aren't getting what they want from the connection then the anger and frustration come back. Inside there is an intense fear of being lonely and being abandoned but on the outside, the individual just feels pure anger. Some people diagnosed with borderline personality disorder can't comprehend how to control their rage and anger, so some take it to a physical level with their significant other. Studies done have shown that people with BPD are related to being aggressive towards your partner, physically, emotionally, and sexually they are showing their internal anger.

People with BPD really see the world as either everyone is good or everyone is bad. They see the world as a negative place with horrible people or this place where everyone is just trying to live their own life and be grateful that they are still here in this moment. With that perspective that really will change the relationship with your significant other. IF you see all as bad then you will see the negative in your spouse a lot easier than most.

It becomes hard when you are the spouse of someone with BPD. You will want to leave but without realizing it they are using their own manipulation to keep them around. Studies show that men are more emotionally intense than women with borderline personality disorder. They show an increase of jealousy, anger, and depression which are common in these men. But you need to remember that it's not all men with BPD. Some can also be aggressive if they think there is a gap or void in a relationship that doesn't need to be there.

The best thing you can do to start going up in your relationship is counseling and therapy. It sounds like a lot, but if you truly want this person in your life for a long time then you are going to need to put some effort into the relationship. You both can seek different therapists or they can try a conjoined therapy session. Just taking this step is a huge vital step into truly understanding your significant other with borderline personality disorder. If you worked with different therapists first then you could both work on your individual issues before diving into the relationship. Since the rise of supply and demand with BPD counseling, there are plenty therapists out in the world who specialize with BPD patients. Those are the people worth going to because they can teach you more about yourself or if your significant other had BPD they can teach you so much about the disorder.

If you are in a relationship with someone with BPD please go to counseling or just research borderline personality disorder so you can try your hardest to understand what your spouse is going through. It is a hard path but starting with the first step is all you need to worry about.

If pure counseling or therapy doesn't work for yourself or your significant other than you can try numerous options to help. You can go into hospitalization for as long as needed to completely learn about yourself. You could research hospitals that even are drug-free or your religion, you can go anywhere, it doesn't have to be like the movies. If the drug route is your way then you could talk to your therapist about what medications could work for you. Medicine helps balance out your internal chemical wheel and can definitely work for some people. If drugs are part of the reason you are going down in the relationship or in life then you can try substance abuse treatment.

You can learn about how to function without those extra additives in life. You can help become a purer version of you, your child state form of yourself. They even have support groups for your loved ones to take if they wanted to. Those can help you understand that you aren't alone with this and you can expand your knowledge on the subject of borderline personality disorder.

10

Stories About People with BPD That Overcome It All

There are many different types of people that have BPD and most react differently to situations. Some people overcome the disorder and can still live normal lives that some people probably would never tell that they had BPD. Now there are others, who can't cope with their disorder and they let it take them over. Most people are like this within the slightest during their first stages of diagnosis. You don't really understand why you are the way that you are, but you will slowly understand it and overcome your situation. So many people in the past have had BPD and they are still here within their own stories to tell us what they did to overcome it all. It is a song challenge for yourself, but once you have accepted it and started working towards a better you then you will see the progress. I swear in the end its worth it to grab a hold of your disorder so you are in control, not the other way around.

If you are a loved one or a friend than this story is meant to help you. It isn't just about the person with BPD because all of the family has to be around them all the time, so you should learn how to deal with your family member so you can be more aware. Just like this man and his BPD wife.

She had BPD and it made her fall into a downward spiral. There were countless police charges and suicide attempts, so that included many institutional visits. Her husband tried following her around like a pet just trying to help wherever he can, but he realized too far in that he was trying to help in all the wrong ways. He was always trying to help her, not focusing on the pain that he and his 3 kids were going through. He didn't realize that she is the only one who can really help herself and she needs to figure out this part of her life on her own. Then he finally just looked at himself, instead of just focusing on the BPD he saw himself. He realized that this is almost as hard on him as a wife. He started to go to non-BPD therapies and express his emotions on the matter. He always wondered why he should put up with this abuse, what he should do to help his kids not suffer, and slowly seeing his life die infant of his eyes. Therapy was the best decision in the world, it helped this man regain some of his strength that he had lost before.

He stood up to his wife and told her either he leaves with the kids or she leaves for extensive therapy. He took a bold move because he genuinely cares about this relationship. You can see that she does too and she did not want to get a divorce, so she went off to a 16-week therapy. That therapy was DBT and CBT based, with no drugs given at all. In that time period, her husband worked on himself and realized all the things he was doing to "help" her that was eventually "hurting" her. To this day, when she comes back from therapy, their whole family is stronger for it. They were all happy because they knew how well she did at therapy. There's obviously still going to be some moments, but they never escalate past that. That was one of the main issues of before. The moral of the story is to always work on yourself, always accept what is coming to you, give everyone a choice, and stand your ground. Good luck to you all.

If you are one of many people in this world and you have Borderline Personality Disorder, the first step you are taking to research is outstanding. Learning about your disorder will not happen overnight, like any other subject there are just too many branches that come off of the truck. You can start to learn about something and then realize that it just goes deeper and deeper into the subject. It will take some time, probably years, but you will find yourself at the end of all of this. You just really need to have the desire to do it. Here's a story of a man who successfully overcame his disorder, just some inspiration to everyone reading this.

You have to remember before reading this story that your problems aren't going to magically go away. The more success stories you read the more you come to the fact that this all shouldn't be so linear. No matter where you are in your stage of accepting yourself you will always have ups and downs. At the end stage of your acceptance, you will still have those down moments. The struggle only just gets easier, but you have to remember that it will always be there. This man is in his mid-20's and diagnosed 7 years ago. The day he got diagnosed he rushed home to research literally every end of what he had.

This man became ecstatic because he now knew the explanation of all his problems. He thought maybe he wasn't a bad person or that things aren't always his fault like people told him countlessly and made him believe it. He finally saw his opening to get better, to be more like the rest. Sadly, a couple years later there was a social stigma around the world that having a mental illness is horrible. Everyone around him was saying he just hid behind his diagnosis and just used the disorder as an excuse for bad behavior. He ended up thinking that of himself because that's all he was getting out of people. In these moments, he thought about all the steps he has taken so far, and they all just meant nothing. It's like square one again. Every feeling of worthlessness and doubt came back in my mind full swing. He quit his hobbies, he quit writing, and just though little of himself again.

It felt like he couldn't do anything to positively impact himself or his family because of what has happened in the past. Most of his family members don't believe in his diagnosis and his friends all eventually end up leaving because of short moments of time where he wasn't in control of his emotions. I never blamed anyone for not wanting to be near or around me, but not having a support system was breaking him. Even though he lives at his father's house, he barely speaks to him. He is just always scared of the awful words that will slip out of his mouth next. Every single part of his surroundings left him feeling like there was no hope because there was always no help. Nobody wanted a man like him in their life, someone with all these questionable actions in the past.

The turning point was when he ended up reading a book that overall taught him that there are actually good people in this world. It showed that some people always want to help, they are willing and even eager for the chance, and just that made him smile. He has to have frequent reminders of this because the people around and his internal self, are making him lose faith in all of the humanity and shatter all his hopes. All he wants is for people to show love in this world because humanity can be pretty beautiful if we all tried. Those strong emotions you feel when you first fall in love or when you are at the peak of your anger are wrong emotions that people with BPD have to deal with on a day to day basis.

Now if you take those emotions up 10 notches that that is what someone with BPD calls intense emotions. Your emotions can become unbearable fast because the BPD kicks in. You can't control your mind, your body, or your speech. It can take over and say or do things that you will end up regretting deeply but you will always have to live with it. People will assume it was your fault because that's what their perspective can see, they will never know how hard you fought to keep control. It's very easy to feel helpless and very hopeless, thinking there is nothing to completely fix you.

You think of yourself as completely toxic and that is a very toxic thought to have about yourself. You need to control your emotions or you will be lead to damaged relationships, people walking away, and ends up causing you abandonment issues in the process. It is a cycle of negativity that only you can break.

The turning point to all of this is people around the world need to be aware of the words they say to anyone, especially people with mental illnesses, beach it is damaging and it sticks with a person. The people in this world that are aware and actually care are the ones you need in your life. You need pushes up in the world not down. He feels helpless but truly doesn't want the whole world to be in the same boat. All this man wants you to grab from this story is if you have BPD then it's not your fault and there are people out there who are willing to be there for you, people who genuinely care about you.

If you don't have BPD and you are reading this, think before you speak. I know everyone reading this has some negative comment someone has said about you years and years ago, but can't remember who was the last person to say something nice to you. Fix the problem don't just be the problem. Some people in this world are genuine and some aren't, its sadly the way that the world turns. You can't have one without the other, but if you are surrounded by negativity all the time every day and you have BPD, I swear you should find new people and you will forever be, please.

You will still have your moments and your outbursts, but they can be contained to a minimal. Positive help and positive thinking can really make you go far with your lives journey. I believe that every single person who has BPD can make a better version of themselves that they can actually enjoy. You all are amazing human beings, it just matters if your watering and feeding the positivity plant or the negativity plant. It's always your choice.

PART II

Chapter 1: We are social animals

As Aristotle said, humans are social animals. This was the first notion that I came across when I started my journey to become a better social player and increase my social skills. However, one question kept arising in my head. If we are truly social animals, why is it so hard for so many people to convey their message without turning red or start shaking? I decided that "shyness" was not a satisfying answer and started digging deeper. I found out that, over time, several factors may justify a difficulty in this area. Here are the most common ones:

1.   1.   Inadequate learning of social skills can be determined by the impossibility of observing adults who surround us—sufficiently effectively and protracted over time—or who surrounds us and shapes our education also has difficulty confronting social situations. As a result, the skills that are necessary cannot be acquired. Why? Because we learn by emulating others and if there is a lack of practical examples, there is no way we are able to get social practices in our system.

1.   2.   There is a lack of positive reinforcement from the surrounding environment. This can be linked to the lack of both valid social contacts and positive feedback that are necessary for the development and consolidation of social skills.

1.   3.   A symptom characterized by social anxiety that can reach an intensity that prevents the subject from using all or part of his abilities. This is why having social troubles does not correspond

with being ignorant or not having anything to say. The content is there; it is just difficult to pull it out.

4.   4.   The presence of side effects of drugs that can make it difficult to approach social situations. In fact, even if most people think that alcohol can help them become better social players, it is a game that does not last for a very long time. In fact, even if it is true that drinking makes anyone more sociable, it is also true that after the effect has gone away, the insecurity begins to increase. I strongly recommend staying away from alcohol and drugs, especially when working on social skills.

At this point, I was wondering: what can I do to improve my social skills? I knew that there was a way. I just had not found it yet. Then something changed.

I started taking courses on how to date women and know more people. Day after day, month after month, I began to see tangible progress and, soon enough, I became a strong social player. In the next chapters, I will discuss the main strategies I have applied to transform who I was.

Chapter 2: What are social skills?

Social skills are those skills that we use every day in life to communicate and interact with other people, both individually and in groups.

People with strong social skills are usually more successful in both professional and personal life because they move well in a team and are able to communicate effectively with other people. Having suffered from social anxiety, I know that hurts, but it is just the truth.

A person (or a leader) who is good at these skills is basically a great communicator.

Social skills are the culmination of other dimensions of emotional intelligence. Social skills move people to go in the direction they want, with the strong awareness that nothing important is done alone, but teamwork and community effort is fundamental.

What I discovered is that social skills can be divided into two groups:

1.   1.   the skills that influence people, such as influence, communication, conflict management, inspiration, and change;

1.   2.   the skills that generate collaboration, such as knowing how to build bonds, collaboration, and knowing how to work in a team.

It's never too late to improve your social skills (I started at the age of 40). The first step is to honestly examine yourself and admit that you need to improve in your deficient areas.

Let's find out some tips that will help you do it.

Chapter 3: Nine Strategies to Improve your social skills

During my researches, I discovered that there were essentially nine strategies that successful people applied to be a great social player. I started practicing them all, one after the other. I strongly believe that anyone can become a good social actor, but only with the right guidance. Even if at the beginning it might be a struggle, when you start seeing your life to change in every aspect, a strong motivation will kick in and drag you forward. In fact, I discovered that there is a relevant correspondence between the ability to socialize and success in other aspects of life. For instance, good social skills make it simpler to influence people and make new friends, craft powerful and long-lasting relationship, and climb the corporate ladder.

If you feel or know that you are not a very social person, it is fundamental to study how to build this aspect of your character. Here are the nine strategies that will help you get started on your journey.

1. Learn how to Listen

People are often centered on themselves, and because of this, many are used to not allow the other person to have their turn to speak. This can result in a frustrating situation, where the other interlocutor perceives you as rude.

I, too, often did it and maybe I will do it again in the future. But once I started to try to focus my mind on the other person by forgetting about myself, being able to feel better what other people say or want to say, everything started to change for the better. Suddenly, I was able to offer

better advice, enjoy the conversation much more, and build stronger relationships. One trick that I used was to look at the mouth of the other person. In this way, I was focusing all my energy to the point where their voice was coming from. This allowed me to exclude any distraction and get more inside their point of view. It is a great social practice and I recommend you to try it out.

2. Be really *interested in other people*

If you start paying more attention towards other people, you will be naturally perceived as a better individual. Furthermore, this will allow you to become a better listener as well since you will get deeper into other people's feelings and points of view.

Only by opening your heart and truly listening to what other individuals want to tell you will you discover that everyone has something interesting to say. We often get too picky in what we like to talk about and that we totally exclude certain topics from our daily conversations. However, by confronting them, you will improve your social skills for sure.

When I first stumbled upon this tactic, I did not understand it fully. In fact, most people are interested in others in a fake way, which does not lead very far. Only by truly caring about other people will you be able to become a better listener. Of course, you cannot care about everyone in the same manner, so start by meeting people with the same interests you have: it will make the practice much easier.

3. Treat others how you would like to be treated

The law of reciprocity is a paradigmatic expression of how the world works. In fact, the way you treat someone else is the way he will be obliged to treat you. Karma may take some time to kick in, but rest assured that you will be rewarded for your kind actions. Furthermore, being kind has an amazing social impact on other people.

"Being one" is one of the most important aspects when it comes to social skills. Only by being aligned in everything you do will you become a better social player.

4. Keep a positive attitude

Having a positive attitude is a decision, not a coincidence. In fact, you may have noticed that there are people who are always calm and cool, while others tend to get caught up in situations. You may not be able to do it all the time, but keeping a positive attitude is something that can be learned and "installed" in your mental system. Everyone likes positive people, so do not overlook this important social treat. When a problem arises, before focusing on the bad side, and with proper exercise, you will begin to see opportunities and what's good in any person or situation.

Obviously, this does not mean you should avoid difficult conversations or skip through issues when other people bring them up. However, you can influence the course of the discussion by sharing positive points of view and helping others to not give up. By doing so, you will become "the positive guy," which is a great social role to play.

5. Be silent and speak less

At first, when I was trying to improve my social skills, I thought that, in order to practice, I had to talk all the time. However, I discovered that there are certain interesting advantages in being a much quieter person. First of all, being silent is a great way to work on your listening skills and avoid unnecessary fights, reducing the possibility of a falling out that may arise from you criticizing them (even if you do not mean to). Especially if you are facing a topic that you do not know too much about, let the other person carry on the conversation and just go with the flow, adding appropriate and valuable comments from time to time.

6. Communicate more than with your words

To become a better communicator you have to improve the way you say something, filling up your words with physical excitement and tangible passion.

Your attitude, as previously stated, can physically modify your body, making you look more open or close, depending on your emotions. For example, if you are feeling calm, open, and relaxed, this will be expressed by your body and vice versa. When you listen, for example, you can keep a passionate eye contact with the other interlocutor to transmit the sensation that you are actually listening to him.

Learning and understanding body language is a great tool in your arsenal and something that I highly encourage you to develop.

7. Break the ice effectively.

When you first meet a new person, I suggest you begin with a generic topic, rather than a personal one. You can talk about current events,

comment on the weather, a compliment, or an observation. To chat is not always easy. In fact, it can happen to go into the ball and not know what to say. Here are some practical ideas that have helped me in many situations:

- • "I like your hat. Where did you buy it?"

- • "The climate is really crazy. What do you think is going on?"

- • "I like a lot the view from here! What do you think about it?"

- • "These lessons are really interesting, don't you think?"

- ### 8. *Find ways to prolong the conversation.*

After breaking the ice with general topics such as current events or the weather, try to go a bit more on the personal side of things. Ask questions about family, work or personal ideas can stimulate and deepen a dialogue. Remember that you need at least two people to talk, so do not talk too much or too little. Ask open-ended questions, such as those beginning with "Come," "Why," and "What," rather than a closed answer. Here are some ideas to stimulate conversation progress:

- • "So, what's your job?"

- • "Tell me a little bit more about your family."

- • "How did you meet the landlord?"

- • "How long have you been going to this place / Do you practice this activity?"

- • "Do you have any plans for the bridge?"

By asking questions you let the other people "do the job" and you can practice active listening (remember strategy number one?).

9. Avoid delicate subjects with strangers

At first, I thought that by bringing up "heavy topics" I would be seen as the intelligent guy. However, I heard on my behalf that when you break the ice with someone you do not know well, you should avoid certain issues such as disputes over religion, politics, race, and sexual orientation. For example:

- • You can ask a general question about the elections, but it is often considered inappropriate to ask someone who they will vote for.

•   •   You can ask generic questions about a person's religious faith, but there is no need to deepen the ideas that a religion has on matters such as sex.

These are the nine strategies that have allowed me to work on my social skills and become a better communicator. As I have told already, practice is the secret. Get yourself in social situations and start applying them. You will be amazed by the quick progress you will be able to make.

PART III

Chapter 1: Who are you talking to?

For our purposes, a conversation is an exchange of verbally communicated ideas between two people. One of them is you, and the other is someone else. What is the degree of familiarity? Is it someone you've known all your life or is it that new co-worker that has been in the office for only a week? The relationship between those in the conversation helps establish a logical starting point.

An exchange between people who have only known each other professionally usually begins more formally than talk between two people who only know each other outside of their professional lives. It's appropriate to have 'small talk' precede the main focus in professional conversations due to the fact that people don't interact as often when this is the nature of the relationship and there are more uncertainties about one another.

With respect to personal relationships, there is a difference between what we shall call simple relationships and invested relationships. Because relationships have the potential to evolve, connections might be transitioning from simple to a more complex relationship such as that of a someone we've started to date or perhaps a new mother-in-law. In instances of changing connections, the capital and the stakes of conversations usually increase in value.

Certainly there are instances where two people are connected both personally and professionally, sometimes for a long period of time. Playing golf with business partners is a scenario that could lead to such a situation. This can be a little complicated, and one or both may tend

to suspend the rules of engagement due to familiarity. This may require backing up and trying to have more formally constructed conversation.

If the person you're conversing with is someone new to you, it's really important to know yourself well and be aware of any personal tendencies or personality traits that might be perceived as 'a bit much' until others get to know you. Most of us can think of a personality quirk for just about anybody we know, including ourselves. Others who know us well have likely offered constructive criticism of the more challenging aspects of our personality and we should take this to heart.

Chapter 2: What are your motivations?

Any conversation has a purpose. Perhaps it is simply to maintain good relations in an established friendship. We engage in many conversations with no real purpose or objective in mind other than to maintain connection a light-hearted connection – as in the one we have perhaps with someone who we encounter once a week or so that works the check-out line in the grocery store.

Conversations don't always have a destination to be reached or some other tangible outcome, depending upon the nature of the relationship. Simple relationships such as with someone working the check-out line with who we might have a brief conversation in passing are quite different from more invested relationships, such as that with a romantic companion, relative, or professional colleague. Our motivations for engagement vary here and we need to have at least a small appreciation for the purpose, lest we lose track of what we might have invested.

Romantic and business conversations, different as they may be in terms of topics, tone, and other attributes of communication do have in common that we are talking about some level of investment on our part and presumably on the part of someone else as well. Whether it's someone we're thinking about proposing marriage or a merger, there's a lot of investment in either case.

All invested conversations require that the wants, needs, and demands of one person be measured alongside those of the other. Are you asking someone to help your business grow by offering an innovative analysis of sales data? Are you persuading your spouse that it's time for the family to grow with the addition of another child? An inventory will

need to be taken in either scenario of the points that are shared in addition to where there are differences. Unless something goes terribly wrong and invested relationships dissolve, conversations will continue to occur and should reflect an effort on the part of two people to recall and maintain an awareness of what they are asking of each other.

Chapter 3: How will you prepare?

When a meeting is scheduled or a date is on the calendar, there is often much anticipation about how things will go. Anticipation leads to expectation or in some cases, reservation. Going over the possible outcomes in your mind followed up by a rehearsal or mock conversation is a good way to cover your bases and provide a sense of confidence about the impending conversation. If someone else is not available, read a dialogue with several exchanges as means to warm up before the actual conversation takes place

A number of variables can come into play that would affect preparation. A lot depends on whether the conversation taking place is between people in a new versus existing relationship. If the other person is new to you, other than being resourceful and gleaning some pertinent facts for conversation fodder, about all you can do is have some topics in mind in the event that the conversation stalls.

If you have the benefit of having past conversations with someone, this is helpful in that you can recall how that person tends to engage with you. Will they lead the conversation if you give them the chance or will they defer? In the cases where there is familiarity, more preparation will have to be put into a conversation that is anticipated to be strained. For instance, if conflict resolution is a likely aspect, think of appropriate questions ahead of time and ways to address issues that diffuse tension, and create a more relaxed environment. Think about acknowledging differences up front using a reconciliatory tone.

Chapter 4: Which tactics are indispensable?

So we're at the point where introductions and small talk are over. From start to end, there are multiple tactics than can be employed to enhance the outcome, much like playing a hand of cards in a timely fashion.

Starting a conversation in amicable fashion is critical. Cut the small talk short or eliminate it if the other person is short on time or simply prefers to get down to business in short order. If it is your first conversation with someone, be mindful that you never get a second chance to make a first impression, and that impression, be it fair or not, may be formed very quickly. Early on acknowledge the other party's interests or concerns prior to stating your own, if you are the one to open things up or lead the conversation.

From start to finish, be constantly mindful and feel things out on everything from the tone of the conversation to how the other person is reacting. If a conversation gets out of hand or veers off course very far, it may be difficult to achieve the original goals that were set out. Quietly ask yourself "is everything going well, or should I try to make an adjustment?" If the other person stumbles or seems confused about how things are proceeding, try to improve clarity so that both of you are confident about how things are going relative to what might have been anticipated.

Being perceived as focused and giving the other person your full attention is perhaps the most important characteristic of someone who has productive conversations. If you come across as aloof or distracted it will probably be a downer. Someone may have taken a significant chunk of time out of their day to set aside for what they thought was

going to be a meaningful exchange and instead they are totally deflated by someone who seems somewhere else.

We have already shed light on coming up with appropriate questions in advance for what are anticipated to be challenging conversations. This is particularly true if modern electronic communication or social media exchanges have preceded or led to the conversation. Incomplete thoughts or confusion created by these shorthand approaches to communicating may result in questions that should be dealt with at the beginning of the conversation. Heck, they may be the entire reason for the conversation. Giving prior thought to appropriate questions is good in any case as the most relevant questions may not come to mind if you wait until the conversation has begun. It is likely that the most curious questions, which reflect serious thought on your part, will come up in advance. Modify questions if you perhaps initially asked something too broad.

Maintain composure rather than get defensive when someone is confrontational or insulting. Disarming someone with a witty or playful response give you the control that they forfeited by deploying counterproductive language.

Give thorough responses that indicate you have respect for other peoples' questions. Abbreviated or literal responses in addition to being insufficiently clear, may also suggest a lack of respect or consideration for what the other person is trying to learn. If their facial expression or other observable response suggests that they did not get the information they were wanting, politely ask them to clarify what they were asking for if it is not abundantly clear.

Be mindful of where the conversation is going and be ready to get it back on track if it is headed into unproductive or counterproductive turf. Be prepared to usurp the role of leading the conversation should it stall. The other person might not be inclined to take the initiative here, and you may have no way of knowing if they're new to you.

Just like you shouldn't give a literal or abbreviated response, you shouldn't ask questions that would lead someone to think you were asking for such. Questions that demand responses beyond the mundane will give the other person a chance to share a more detailed account leaving them feeling as though they got to share the whole story.

People want to be recognized and given due credit. Do yourself a favor and take the opportunity in advance. If they feel the need to bring attention to an accomplishment before you mention it, they are indicating that they feel a lack of respect. Recognition will make future conversations more productive because validation will motivate people to be more engaged.

We need to listen effectively in order to gain the respect of those we engage in conversation. Constantly cutting them off or interrupting them will make it seem as we are dismissing their importance in the relationship. One is not listening effectively if they are unable to stay in the present moment. Diverting the conversation may also be regarded as not respecting someone's concern about the topic at hand.

Making demands or requests in a conversation is a sensitive matter. Be fair and don't ask for too much. Don't ask for something if it is going to be obvious that you haven't done anything to help yourself and just want to place a burden on the other person. No one wants to feel as

though they're being taken advantage of, so consider carefully as to whether you should make a request of them.

Demonstrate that you are in the moment by actions that are visibly obvious. Record notes during the conversation or commitments you have made. Place a future date on your phone calendar when an event is mentioned. This implies intent on your part to follow through and makes the other person feel as though they've gotten something across to you and that their input was worthwhile.

Chapter 5: The Supreme Tactic – The Follow-Up Conversation

After a conversation, you must take inventory of how things went. If you know of strategic mistakes that were made along the way, make note of them and take care not to commit them in future conversations. You must hold yourself responsible for being able to recall any specific outcomes and good note-taking is the best way to accomplish this. If a conversation ends with both parties knowing what was specifically agreed to or are certain of specific commitments that were made and how outcomes are to be achieved, it may not be necessary to revisit the conversation down the road. When outcomes aren't certain and nothing was specifically agreed upon, it may be in the best interest of two people to come back together and express their views about what each took from the conversation. Revisit the points of agreement and disagreement with emphasis given as to why sentiments differed on particular subjects that were discussed. An apologetic tone might be called for if you lost your composure or you felt deficient in attention or focus. Remember that follow-up conversation may be used as a polite gesture to offer thanks or appreciation, in which case they needn't be extended affairs. If a follow-up is something of an in-between linking two major conversations, it may require more input as it establishes what will be discussed in the latter conversation.

PART IV

Chapter 1: How Technology Has Affected Our

Communication Skills

Before we dive into the practical strategies of overcoming those dreaded awkward moments, there is some basic information that you should know. You see, it is my belief that seeing a full picture of the context will help you to understand the basis of your communication block better.

In truth, the world we live in today is a lot different than it used to be back in the days of covered wagons and community bathing. Yuck! It is certainly better in a myriad of ways. We have the technology, fast cars, airplanes, hell even indoor plumbing! But. Just but. It isn't better in some respects.

We Were Set Up To Fail

You see, people call this the age of communication. People call this the golden era of instant connectivity based on the ease in which we can talk to people hundreds or even thousands of miles away from us. That is certainly a great thing in all but wait. What about the people that are sitting right next to us? How connected to them are we?

Over seventy percent of the world's population admits to having a problem with communicating properly with people in their families. Think about that for a moment. SEVENTY PERCENT! That is just mind boggling. And to put things into perspective, more than three out of four of your neighbors probably face this same issue as you do.

It is also faithful to a vast extent that a consequence of that problem leads to one not having the proper communication skills to engage on a personal level with strangers or primary acquaintances.

Have you noticed that in the past, before telephones were in every household, it was so much easier to talk to people face to face? That is because for the longest time, excluding the post that came every week or the occasional messenger pigeon that often took days to reach a destination seventy miles away, it was the **only** form of communication with someone! If you wanted to have a full conversation in real time with someone you knew that wasn't living in your own home you had to move your butt up from your seat, walk over to their house, knock on their door, open your mouth, and talk to them. Sounds harsh eh? Now think how many people do that now in the modern age.

This meant that communication was futile to survival in the past. If you needed something from someone, you had to physically and verbally ask for it. This also meant that you would have to communicate regularly with everyone around you to get stuff done.

Past Customs Allowed For Natural Conversations

In the past, it was customary to greet everyone with a smile when you're walking down the street. Not doing so was considered bad manners. In contrast, people living in the modern age are so glued to their smartphones or listening to their music with earphones shoved deep down their ear drums that their mouths don't even move much anymore. People are LESS connected to one another today.

In the past humans had to interact by speaking several times a day and as a result, people were not only more friendly to one another, they became more fluent and natural at talking and communicating with their peers. They had proper training on a daily basis just by opening their mouths more often. How easy is that?

We Were Not Given The Chance To Develop Our Social Skills

You see, children in days gone by were taught from a young age how to socialize. They were sent outside to make their friends, and they were taught how to be self-sufficient. This gave them the confidence to speak to others. In school, they were instructed on what appropriate conversation was. Children were often taught not to speak unless spoken to. This was to teach them to listen to those around them truly and to respond in a meaningful and understanding way. This training not only made them good listeners but also compassionate adults that were able to hold productive conversations in the highest of social settings. As you can see, a conversation was key to survival.

Where's The Social Gathering In The Modern Age?

Let's face it. We are all glued to our smartphones, tablets, and computers. Swiping left on Tinder, surfing the net, texting people on Facebook or iMessage. When have we ever had a decent conversation or a happy get-together with our closest friends? The truth is that we were crippled by our devices the day we got them. It is unfortunate now, isn't it?

Consequences Of Rapid Development

The hectic life and "connectivity" today has turned our society a complete one hundred and eighty degrees. We have started to take for granted the most straightforward and efficient tools for communication and replaced them with devices that we THINK are doing a better job for us. In reality people today are more closed off than they ever were and that is unfortunate. Modernization and technology have robbed us of our most core competencies, and we need to claim it back!

The Intricate Things We ARE Deprived Of:

- The gatherings with friends and family

- The lack of fun festivities

- The missing social events

- The community spirit and comradery with our peers.

- The treatment of everyone around you with respect and dignity that you wish you received.

- The Communication with our neighbors.

Possible Causes

There are many possible reasons for this silence struck pandemic. Most of it can be attributed to one or more of the many technological advances that we have seen over the years. No one person has been able to pinpoint exactly what it is that has changed the friendly ways of the world. Here are some of the possible causes. You can try to decide for yourself what you think has been the downfall of communication.

- **1.** **The Telephone**: The invention of the phone made it easier to take the human element out of a conversation. Instead of going to someone's house every so often and staying a few hours, and having a meal, they could call to say what needed to be said, and then cut the conversation short with the excuse that they were wracking up too many minutes that month. They didn't have to stay on the phone yacking for hours on end because the person on the other end of the line agreed and hung up as well.

The telephone, back when it was invented, was so expensive that only the rich people and government agencies owned them. Created in 1876 by Alexander Graham-Bell, it was the most technologically advanced thing since the dawn of electricity. In the beginning, it cost over a thousand dollars to own a single phone. To make a call, Bell Telephone Industries charged a dollar a minute to dispatch that call. That was a lot of money considering the average worker was lucky to make fifty cents an hour. One minute call time would have been two hours wages, so most average salary households did not have a telephone in the house. That was until the early 1900's after Henry Ford invented the concept of mass production. A company made a telephone that was way cheaper than Bell Industries old phone design, and they found a better way to dispatch calls to make the calls cheaper. During this time, wages went up a lot as well. By this period the minimum wage was about two dollars an hour. This made phones more common in average households. By the nineteen seventies, a home phone was a staple in each house and calls only cost ten cents a minute. This was a great thing, as, by

this time, wages were up to seven dollars an hour for minimum wage. The company that was instrumental in lowering the price of the phone? Well, these days it's known as AT&T.

Due to its cost, the telephone may not have been the downfall of modern communication, but it definitely could have had a hand in it. Particularly as it became easier, and cheaper to purchase. People called rather than stopped by, and these calls did not have to drone on and on, as time was money. This allowed conversations to become shorter, and it made its way into everyday life as well.

- **2.** **Television:** The television was a lot cheaper than the telephone was. It was also a way to get the news a lot easier, as you didn't have to wait until a friend heard something and get back to you. There were also some good programs to watch during the day that entertained people. This entertainment made them want to stay inside and watch it all day. Well, the adults at least. Children were still sent outside to play.

The original television was black and white and only had three channels. It was small and could sit on the dining room table. Brand new, they cost about three hundred dollars, and they had long rabbit ear antennas. In the beginning, this was the only option you had, but as time went on, there were bigger console televisions available. Eventually, the color television was introduced, and some time after that, more channels were added, as cable became a thing. More and more time was spent inside watching TV. Not just by adults anymore, either.

Children were inside more often and watched shows that were geared towards their age groups. People went out and mingled with their neighbors less and less.

Television alone probably was not the downfall of the communication era, but it was a precedent to it. A lot of people began staying inside to watch their soaps instead of going outside to spend time with actual people. For the longest time, children were still sent out to play while the parents watched TV, but as the parents moved to colored cable, the children got the still working black and white rabbit-eared television, and the trend progressed as in the older days, television sets lasted forever.

- **3.** **Game Consoles:** Today there are several hi-tech game consoles out there for people to choose from, and they are often played for hours on end, while the player ignores the outside world. Back when they were first invented, they were a lot different, but no less desirable. They were the envy of every household, and a child that had one was instantly familiar, but he never used that popularity because he was too busy inside playing his new game. When the original Atari came out, it was the sensation that swept the nation.

The first ever game console was nothing like the ones we have today. They took a lot more effort to play. To make a single move, you had to write a program first. This was difficult, but the kids in those days didn't mind, as to them it was a game console, and that was the coolest thing they had ever seen. They

also learned about computer programming before home computers were a thing. As time progressed, the programs were written into the game at production, so all kids had to do was play the game. They also went from almost fifteen hundred dollars to a hundred and fifty dollars. While that was still pretty expensive, it was a lot more affordable than the Atari. The most popular and innovative of these new consoles? The Nintendo Entertainment System, or NES for short. It was the console that every kid wanted, and most kids were able to get for Christmas or their birthday. With the debut of the game Super Mario Brothers stepping away from the typical games of Pong and Galactica, this thrilling console had kids of all ages, and even adults gathered around it to enjoy it. This further engulfed them into their anti-social bubbles as they were too engrossed in the games to go outside.

Video Games are blamed by many as being the downfall of modern society. That can be seen as accurate, as there were so many people beginning to stay indoors rather than going outside. However, there were plenty of friendly people left in the world, and people still visited one another, so is this the truth? Maybe as they progressed, but it was not an immediate destruction.

• 4. **Media:** This one can be brutal. People are so easily influenced by the media, that they could tell the people that Donald Trump farted unicorns, and they would almost believe it. Okay, maybe not that sorry, but that is the general idea with the media. Nowadays, the media is filled with bombings, kidnappings and

other fear mongering materials that it makes it hard to trust the people around you.

In the beginning, the news just stated that. The news. It gave news of the war if there was one, and news With all the fear-inducing news, it makes it hard to want to even talk to anyone, because it seems as if everyone is a murderer now. This is not a conducive environment like friendly ways of the past.

Media could be considered the downfall of the friendly atmosphere, as it seeds fear of the human race in your mind, and that is what seems to have closed people off from their natural chatty instincts.

- **5.** **Internet:** The dawn of the web saw a rise in introverts massively. It is no secret that the web has taken over the minds of most of our youth. This goes hand in hand with the media, as it is the primary source of all media output.

So those are some of the possible causes of why it is harder now to talk to people than it used to be. Of course, for some people, it is more difficult than others. Individuals with anxiety or shyness have a hard time even talking to people that are deemed safe by people they trust. It isn't caused by fear, just a nervousness that causes these people to clam up. Chances are since you are reading this, you are one of these people.

Do not fret. This book will help you get through this. However, be prepared. Sometimes it takes more than self-help, and if your problem has deeper seated issues, you may want to get the help of a psychiatrist. If these tips do not help, it is best to seek the help of one if you wish to be more of a conversationalist, and it is essential for your mental and emotional health. There will be more on that at the end of this book.

Chapter 2: Conversation Tips

Step One-Talking to Yourself

This may seem a little silly, but it does help. It is the easiest way to get over your shyness, as it is more awkward to talk to yourself than it is to talk to other people. You just have to get past the first hump of not wanting to look like a fool and own it.

Go into a room with a mirror, start by offering your hand to shake and mime shaking hands with the person staring back at you while introducing yourself. This may feel a little weird, as there is not going to be a meeting of hands, due to you only having the conversation with yourself.

Once you get past the standard greeting, it is time to hold a conversation. You can either say your mirrored self's responses, or you can keep them in your head. This is where it can get tricky. You cannot think of specific to you answers, rather, you have to think of general answers, as you are not the person you are talking to. Talk away as if an actual person was holding a conversation with you. You can think of this as a live diary, but more civilized and social, as you don't want to spill your secrets to someone who is mostly standing in as a stranger.

Here is a little scenario to help you visualize what it would be like.

SCENARIO

Kelly had just finished reading *How to Talk to Anyone: Ten Secrets You Wish You Knew*, and she wanted to try out the first tip, which was called "Talking to Yourself." She stepped into her bathroom and closed the door.

"Okay, Kelly. You can do this. You have to become better at holding a conversation, as your husband's job requires you to attend various social events with him."

Looking into the mirror she offered her hand to the cold glass, feeling slightly foolish.

"Hello, my name is Kelly. And you are?"

In her head, she planned the response.

I am Richard Simms. A pleasure to meet you, Kelly. She used her husband's boss's name as that was the one she was sure she knew.

"Pleasure to meet you too, sir. How are you and your wife and kids?"

They are doing well, as am I. How about your children?

"Oh, no children yet sir. Wanting to get ahead financially first."

A great plan, I must say. Children are very expensive little buggers.

Kelly was interrupted then, as her husband walked into the bathroom.

"Who on Earth are you talking to?"

"I am practicing holding a conversation. I don't want to embarrass you tomorrow at the banquet." Kelly blushed.

"Awe, sweetheart, you could never embarrass me, but I appreciate the effort, and I am glad you are taking the steps necessary to better yourself. I am proud of you." Her husband kissed her forehead and left.

After that boost of confidence, Kelly found it much easier to practice her conversation skills and felt less awkward about talking to herself in the mirror.

It may seem embarrassing to talk to yourself in a mirror, but after awhile it will be much easier, as you will start to feel better about helping yourself become the best that you can be. If someone comes in and asks you what you are doing, explain to them what you are trying to do. You never know, maybe they will try it for themselves.

Of course, there is still a stigma that talking to yourself means that you are crazy, but once you explain that you are not trying to be weird, you just are trying to become better at conversation, people will understand. It is getting harder and harder for people to hold a normal conversation in this world, so it is always refreshing to hear that someone is trying to better themselves.

Step Two- Have a Few Ice Breakers

It is no secret that after the initial introductions conversation gets awkward if there are no real conversation starters in the room. You say hello, state your name, and ask a few questions about what the person does, and how their day has been, but after that is over, this is when the conversation dies out with a bunch of "Ums" and "Uhhh." Having a few icebreakers is always important as you can keep the conversation going, and often have a few laughs going at the end.

Of course, it is hard to tell exactly what you should use as an icebreaker, and that is why most people have a hard time keeping the conversation going. However, few foolproof icebreakers will make talking to someone a breeze. This section will go over some ice breakers to use...

and some to avoid.

Real Ice Breakers

• **1. Latest viral cat video:** Pretty much everyone in the world loves cat videos, and a lot of people have seen them. Bringing that up in conversation is always a good way of push conversation along. It is a safe topic that won't offend people, and if someone hasn't seen the video, you can show it to them, eliciting a few laughs and smiles. Almost everyone loves cat videos.

• **2. Food:** Everyone eats. So ask the person what kind of food they like. It is always pertinent to ask them first because if they are vegan, you don't want to say "Bacon is the greatest, is it not?" Discuss different cuisines, and if they have not tried one of your favorites, suggest a good place find it. Talking about food can bring people closer together, as they find common likes and interests in cuisines.

• **3. Music:** Everyone listens to music. No matter what their tastes, everyone loves music. You cannot deny the fact that life would be boring without it. It fills the awkward silences, and it can bring up someone who is down. There is no escaping the fact that music is tied to emotions as well. Try asking the person what their favorite song is. Ask them the genres they like. If you find you have some interests that are similar, that is great, and that will further boost the conversation.

- **4.** **Hobbies:** Everyone has a passion that probably has nothing to do with their job. Hobbies are what make life interesting. It is a safe topic to approach because many people love to talk about what they enjoy, but rarely anyone asks.

- **5.** **Anything to do with interests:** Pretty much anything to do with personal interests is safe to talk about because people love to talk about themselves. They like to make known what they enjoy, and they love when someone shows interest in them. However, most people are too shy to talk about themselves unprompted because they do not wish to seem conceited.

Bad Ice Breakers

- **1.** **Politics:** There are so many different opinions out there, and unfortunately with the policy, everyone thinks that they are right. The conversation can get awkward if you are a Democrat butting heads with a Republican. That is only the tip of the iceberg though. Tempers often flare at the slightest mention that either party may be corrupt, so it is best all around to just avoid the conversation entirely.

- **2.** **Religion:** This is another one that is best avoided. Religion is a very sensitive subject for some, and no one wants someone else's religion shoved in their faces. That is why you are better off keeping this one put away.

- **3.** **Life choices:** It is great that you have decided to become a vegan and all, but you do not have to convert everyone who is around you. Same with any of the life choices you make, whether you sell Avon or those scammy weight loss products,

virtually no one wants to hear the spiel. Save it for if you are asked.

So there you have it. Some good and some not-so-good icebreakers to help you extend any conversation past the initial hell0. Once you can establish a gateway to the conversation, you will be able to carry on a lot easier than you would if you had not used an icebreaker at all, and were floundering about like a fish out of water, trying to figure out what to say.

How These Tips Help

These tips help you relax a little bit. They give you a little confidence boost, knowing that you are prepared to hold a conversation with people you may meet because you have practiced the basics. It is a lot easier to do something once you have practiced it a few times.

It also helps you get past the awkwardness, as nothing is more awkward than holding a conversation with yourself. You will be able to talk to someone without feeling silly because you couldn't possibly feel any goofier than you did speak to a mirror.

Follow these tips to get the ball rolling on talking to people.

Chapter 3: Holding a Conversation

Now that you have gotten past the tips on how to approach and talk to someone, it is time to move on to the advice on how to hold a conversation. This is important because starting a conversation is only a small part of the battle. This means that you have to be able to continue a conversation past the point of the icebreaker.

Conversations do not have to be hours long, but you do have to keep them at a length that does not make you seem rude, or disinterested. If you only talk to someone about one subject and then leave, the person will feel as if they did something to offend you or something like that. You do not want to leave anyone feeling that way.

The best way to avoid that is to make sure that you keep the conversation going to the point where it would be safe to exit without offending the person you are talking too. This section will help you more understand how to keep a conversation going and keep it going well.

Tip Three- Self Disclosure

To understand this advice, there is going to have to be some in-depth explanation of what self-disclosure is. To save you from having to look it up, this tip will include all the information you need to know about it. Of course, that will make this trip a lot longer, but it is better to have a long tip that you understand than a short briefing on something that leaves you confused.

Self-disclosure is where you add to a conversation by giving the other person information about yourself. This is a hard thing to do, as most people worry about boring others with talk of themselves, or they are afraid to seem conceited.

There are two dimensions to self-disclosure. They are breadth and depth. These are both essential to holding a good conversation, and connecting with the person you are talking to. You want to be able to connect with the people around you or else you will not be able to hold a genuine and meaningful conversation. You have to have both to enable the act of self-disclosure indeed.

The breadth of self-disclosure refers to the range of topics you discuss when opening up about yourself. No, you don't have to disclose your deepest darkest secrets, but giving someone a little bit of information about several different subjects about yourself allows them to feel a little closer to you, thus enabling them to open up about themselves. This helps extend the conversation and lets the person feel values as if you are interested in talking with them. Try starting with the easiest topics, such as interests, and move on to schooling, and views on the world. The more subjects you cover, the longer the conversation will be, and the more you will be able to connect with the person you are talking too.

Depth is slightly harder to reach. Now if you are just chatting up with someone you don't plan to develop a deep friendship with, you can almost skip depth, but a deep conversation is necessary for those you wish to establish a real friendship with. However, even in a simple conversation, you need to have some depth to what you are saying. Tell

them about the time you broke your arm in third grade, or something of the like. Give them a memory to make them feel as if you care about the conversation you are having, and are not just chatting to pass the time.

The act of self-disclosure is a type of social penetration. This is a theory that you can only establish any relationship, whether it be romantic or platonic, by communication. But not just any type of communication, systematically fluid conversation. This means that over time, you let the person in more and more, and you change the direction of your conversation regularly to establish a connection with the individual you are communicating with.

You also have to allow time for the person to reciprocate in the conversation. Don't spend the entire time talking about yourself. If you are worried about droning on too long about what you like and such, try employing the one detail method. This means that you share a detail about yourself, and let the other person share a detail about themselves. Continue this on until you find a happy medium between not sharing enough and talking too much.

As you can see self-disclosure is critical, as you need to allow, a person to feel as if you are invested in the conversation. If you do not seem like you care to talk to them, they will close off, and not want to talk much more than the basic hello followed by an icebreaker subject. So how do you efficiently employ this technique?

- **1.** **Start Small:** On top of them feeling like you are interested, they also have to be interested in what you have to say. Rather than unloading a whole pile of information on someone that doesn't

care, start with a small bit of information to see if they take the bait. If you use the icebreaker about music, try telling them your favorite song, and explaining a final reason for why you love it. If they just give you a one-word reply, it is best to duck out of the conversation then. They don't care. However, if they seem interested, and ask you, more then you can start talking about more of your interests and such.

- **2.** **Decide on The Type of Conversation:** You should always try to approach every conversation as if you seek to make a new friend. However, if you are at a convention with people from around the globe, chances are you are not going to establish a life-long friendship. You should still show interest in the individual, but that would impact the type of information that you are going to divulge. You don't want someone you are never going to see again knowing a deep secret about you. Instead, tell them about childhood memories that you don't feel would impact how they think of you. Your favorite thing to do as a child or stuff like that. Those are safe subjects for people who you are just talking to at that moment.

- **3.** **Skim the Surface:** You want people to be interested in you for a long time. This means that you cannot divulge everything about you in one conversation. You have to be conservative with your information. The best way to do this is to take a little bit of information from many different subjects to talk about. As you get to know a person more and more, you can add more details to that. This helps you also ensure that you are not talking about yourself too much.

- **4.** **Allow Reciprocation:** The best part of self-disclosure is that it allows the other person a gateway to say themselves as well. You don't want to hog the stage and only talk about yourself. You want to keep the flow of information even. Give the other person some time to tell you about themselves as well. The conversation will come alight as you are swapping stories and some fun little tidbits of information about yourself.

- **5. Be Loose:** Telling someone about yourself should be done with ease. You don't want to sound like someone who is selling something, though in reality that is what you are doing in a way. You are trying to convince the person to like you with the truth. However, it should not sound like you are a documentary. You should be light and airy when talking about yourself. Make the person interested. Intrigue them, and draw them in, get them want to know more about you.

- **6. Timing:** Just like when you deliver the punchline to a joke, it is all about the timing. You have to time the information that you provide. This is a little tricky if you don't know what goes into timing a deliverance. There has to be a level of interest from the other person. To ensure that you have their interest, you have to make them ask a few questions. You can't just offer up all the information. However, you can't make them pry every bit of info from you either. There has to be a give and take kind of flow going on there.

- **7. Caution:** There are some things that you do not tell a person you just met. It may seem like you have known the person

forever, but you still have to use caution when divulging certain things. For example, if you were a former addict, it is best not to mention it unless necessary. You do not want anything to skew how they think of you until they get to know you. If you are confident in yourself, however, then try divulging that info. What you are cautious with depends on you.

There you have it. Self-disclosure at its finest. This is one of the most important things to holding a good conversation. Now, remember, your entire conversation does not have to consist of self-disclosure alone, but throwing in a few facts here and there go a long way. Make sure you utilize this to the fullest advantage possible.

Tip Four- Engage the Other Person Fully

Part of the problem these days is that conversation becomes one sided. Even though both parties are speaking, they are not really in the conversation. They are not properly engaging the other person. This is a big issue when communication relies entirely on both parties being actively involved in the discussion to allow it to succeed. If you are not actively engaging the other person, and not participating yourself, then you will fall flat in the conversation.

First off, how you can be engaged in the conversation better, without taking it over.

- **1.   Actively Listen:** No one wants to feel like they are talking to a brick wall. They want to feel like the person they are talking

121

to is genuinely interested in what they have to say. This means that you have to listen to understand. Today's generation teaches

you to hear the reply, and that is where the problem lies. By only looking to respond, you are not processing what the other person is saying because your mind is on yourself. This is a selfish, bad habit that this day and age has taken to sticking too.

- **2.   Reply with Interest:** Even if you are not quite interested in what the other person is talking about, you should always respond with interest. It is polite, and even though you may not be interested in it now, you might gain some interesting knowledge by listening to what they have to say. You can't just expect everyone to have the same interests as you, and there are probably things that you like that others do not like but they still act like they are at least interested in it, because it is the polite thing to do.

- **3.   Ask Questions:** Asking questions to get more information about what they are talking about shows the other person that you were listening, and that you want to know more. It allows the person to be relieved because then they do not feel like they are boring you with their information. The only way that they know that you are interested is if you are asking questions. Then they know that it is okay to continue talking about the subject they are on.

- **4.   Be THERE:** I know it can be hard if someone is droning on and on about something that you have no interest in, but it is still good etiquette to be there mentally. This means that when someone is talking, don't let your mind go on vacation, and tune the person out because if you are that disinterested in them, it is

more polite to change the subject rather than just leave the conversation mentally.

That is how you can be engaged in a conversation. Following these tips will allow you to breathe easier knowing that you are pleasantly talking to a person, and you won't offend them because you seem disinterested. You just have to practice these things, because sometimes it can be a little tricky.

How to Engage Them

- **1.   Be Interesting:** This does not mean you have to make up stories. It has nothing to do with the information you are giving at all. You just have to deliver it in an interesting way. You could tell someone you climbed Mount Everest on the back of Dwayne Johnson, and if you inform the story in a monotone voice, it will sound dull. It is not what you are saying; it is how you are saying. Tell them your stories as if you were telling them for the first time. Be engaged yourself, and show the person that you want them to talk to you. You want their attention. Only then will you get the attention you so desire.

• **2.** **Leave Openings:** Even without using self-disclosure, you still have to leave openings for the other person to talk, no matter the subject. No one wants to stand there and listen to someone take control of the conversation. You might as well be talking to yourself for that matter. Or to the plant in the corner. You have to let the other person talk as well. A good conversation allows both parties to talk equally and without any hitches. It is

not people talking about everything while the other person stands there and nods.

• **3.** **Allow Questions:** If a person asks a question, don't dodge it. This should not have to be said, but a lot of people avoid questions for fear of sounding conceited, but in truth, you just seem rude. If someone is asking a question, you are not going to sound pretentious by answering it. If you dodge a question, the person will feel as if they offended you, and they will be less likely to stay engaged in the conversation.

That is how you engage someone in conversation. It is a lot easier than staying involved in a discussion as long as they are interested in what is being said. All you have to do is be open and friendly, and let the rest fall into place.

How These Tips Help

These tips are designed to help you keep a conversation going without being nervous. These tips also contribute to improving your communication skills. By using these tips, you will feel more comfortable having a longer conversation with someone that you just met than you would be if you were just trying to find things to talk about.

These tips will give you the boost you need to feel confident in your abilities to talk to people and enjoy the conversation without having to worry every second that you are saying something wrong.

Chapter 4: Getting Through a Conversation

These tips are for what you should do during and after a conversation with someone. They are tips on how to properly act when communicating, as there is often some confusion about what to do especially now that it is no longer a curriculum at school or home. Do not fret. This book will clarify that right up.

Tip Five- Etiquette During a Conversation

It is of utmost importance that you have the proper etiquette when talking to someone. The key to holding a good conversation is not to offend them and to show them that you are a real person to talk to. You want to keep their attention and let them know that they have yours. Otherwise, you will not get very far in the communication realm, as people will not want to talk to you, thinking you are rude.

So it is best to study up on proper etiquette before you put yourself out there. While most of these are common sense, they are in here just in case nerves cause a problem with combining common sense with communication. That is a real issue a lot of people have. They cannot rely on their common sense because they are too nervous to remember to use it.

So here are the etiquette rules to help you out. Remember, a slip up is okay as long as you don't do it continually, but it is best to try to be as clean cut as possible to avoid any issues.

- **1.** **Handshake:** This is the first thing you should do, as you say hello. Unless the person is germaphobic, or you are, not

offering a handshake is considered rude. If you do have a phobia of germs, it is best to explain that as you are saying hello, so there are no misunderstandings. Make sure that they know that you are still pleased to meet them; you just would rather not shake their hand. Most people can be pretty understanding.

The perfect handshake is firm but pliant. You can't grip too tight, because you are not trying to intimidate someone, and a grip too loose makes people feel that you are not that thrilled to meet them, and are only doing so out of necessity. This is not a great first impression, as people want to feel like they are worth getting to know. So it is best to make sure you give a real, genuine handshake.

- **2.** **Eye Contact:** This one is important to maintain from the beginning to end. It is always disconcerting to talk to someone who is looking off into the distance or anywhere else but who is talking to them. (autistic people are not counted in this, nor are the ocularly impaired) Eye contact shows that you are paying attention to them. To show you why eye contact is so important, let us have a mini history lesson.

Back in the time of extreme social hierarchy, where people who made less money than you were deemed undesirable, eye contact was a way of establishing that social ladder. Anyone who was considered below you had to make eye contact with you, while you were not to make eye contact with them. To

make eye contact with a person deemed lowly, put you on their level, and could cause you to lose your social position if caught.

Kings never looked anyone but other kings in the eye, no one ever made eye contact with serfs other than other serfs. Men did not make eye contact with women, as even women were deemed below them. They only time someone made eye contact with a lady that was not another woman, was a servant, or a peasant to a duchess or queen. Eye contact was the primary factor of social hierarchy

By not looking someone in the eye during a conversation, you are essentially saying that they are beneath you and that what they have to say is n't matter. That may not be what you are trying to do, but that is the message you are portraying when you refuse to look someone in the eye.

- 3.   Body Language: This will be more brushed on in a later chapter, but it also falls under etiquette. You have to have an open body language in a conversation. Otherwise, you risk making a person feel as if you are unapproachable, and not open to discussion. You can also make them feel as if what they are saying has no value. You can do so much damage with a few simple gestures, and this is a problem. You have to be careful with your stance and make sure that you are not closing yourself off.

- 4. No Phone: This should go without saying, but if your phone goes off, DON'T ANSWER IT! Society today is so caught up in the conversations that they have going on on the other side of the screen, that they forget the importance of conversation

with the person on the other aspect of the table. You are in a real time conversation with a real person. (Not that the person texting you isn't real, but they are not there.) The best thing to do is to put your phone on silent if you know you are going to talk to people. That way you do not feel tempted to pull it out and text rather than speaking with those around you.

Cell phones are a wonderfully destructive device. They can help you connect with people from around the world, but unfortunately, that causes you to disconnect from the people that are right next to you. A lot of people use their phone as a crutch to not have to talk to people when they feel uncomfortable. This does not help you in any way. They only way to become comfortable with a situation is to put yourself out there and talk to people. Find someone to talk to and eventually you will take your mind off of the fact that you are anxious about being around people.

• 5. Don't Interrupt: When someone is talking to you, it is best to stay quiet until you are sure they have finished what they are saying. You have to be very careful when talking to someone that you are listening to them, and not listening to respond. This is one of the biggest problems in today's conversations. No one looks to people for more than knowing when to jump in and reply. This leads to more people interrupting, which often angers the other person, and makes them not want to talk to you any longer.

Listen to the person, and remember that you would not want to be interrupted. No one likes to be talked over, and no one likes talking to someone who constantly does it. Be patient. Your time to talk will come.

• 6. Personal Space: This is a big one. A lot of people get really close to people when they are talking. This is uncomfortable for the other person. You have to make sure that you keep a safe distance between you and the other person. Arm's length apart is a good chatting distance unless you are in a loud place, and then from forearm length apart is usually as close as you should be. If it is too loud to hear, then you should hold the conversation until you are in a quieter environment.

Claustrophobia is a big problem for a vast majority of a population. Invading someone's personal space can make them very uncomfortable. You have to respect that people need personal space when talking to you. Even if they don't have claustrophobia, it is still gross when someone is so close to you that you can feel their spit as they are talking. Keep the distance.

- 7. Get Close: This may seem to contradict the last statement, but you have to be close enough that it does not look like you are trying to escape the conversation. However, it is not that contradictory. You just have to find a happy medium. You want to be close enough that the other person is not sniffing themselves trying to figure out if it is them, but you have to be far enough away that you are not crowding their personal space.

A good indicator is your arms. Of course, you do not physically stretch them out to see if you are standing close enough, but rather you visualize where you are at. You should never be so close that you have to bend your arm at more than a ninety-degree angle to touch them, but you should not be so far away that when your arms are fully outstretched your palms can't rest on their shoulders. Try to stay in that golden circle of space, and you should be good.

Those are the tips for etiquette during a conversation. Follow these, and you should have no problem with people not wanting to talk to you. You will make the other person feel respected, and that is what you are striving for.

Tip Six- Etiquette When Leaving a Conversation

- 1.   Timing: As stated before, timing is everything when talking to people. You have to be good at your timing and actually, know when to say something when not to say something. In this case, timing has to do with when to exit a conversation. No matter how good a conversation has been, you begin to wear out your welcome. If a person starts to look around or shift about, they are probably ready to go or do something else. This is your cue to end the conversation if they do not. Finish what you were saying, and then use an exit phrase such as "Oh I can't believe how much of your time I have taken! It was so great talking to you I just got swept up at the moment!" Make them feel good while ending the conversation.

- 2.   Ending Phrase: As mentioned in the above bullet, you have to use a good ending phrase to make the person feel as if the conversation end is not their fault, even if it is. Be polite, and make them feel like you were so enthralled by talking to them that you regret having to end the conversation, but you do not want to take up any more of their time. This will make them feel valued, and that will get them want to talk to you again.

- 3.   Ask for Contact Info: If you have the chance of seeing someone again, or just would like to stay in touch, ask if they would like to exchange contact information. If they say yes, go ahead and give them your number and ask for theirs, giving a test call to make sure you input the number right and allowing them to be sure of the same, as the will have your number on the call. If they do not wish to exchange information, do not push. It doesn't mean you did anything wrong; they just may not think that they will see you again. That is okay.

Always ask if they want to exchange information. It is a lot more comfortable for them, as it gives them a little more room to say no without feeling bad. Asking them for their contact information directly does not allow for them to say no without feeling bad because you assumed that they wanted to. Remember, the right conversation does not mean they have to become your best friend. A lot of people get so attached to someone they had a single enthralling conversation with, that they are upset when the person does not want to keep in touch. This is only human nature, as we are designed to communicate for survival. Breaking yourself of this habit will be difficult, but

if you do it, you will be less affected by the rejection you feel when someone does not wish to stay in touch.

- 4. Follow Up: This only refers to people who exchanged info. If they give you their contact information, then text or call them the next day to see how they are doing and let them know that you were serious about wanting to stay in touch. Make the person feel important, but only text once, and let them respond. They might be busy when you try to reach them and will get back to you later.

These are the etiquette rules for ending a conversation. If you use them, you can be confident that you are not leaving someone with awkwardness in the air.

How These Tips Help

These tips give you the boost up in a conversation to show a person that you are respectful, and that you have proper manners. This will make them enjoy talking to you a lot better than if you did not know these rules.

Etiquette is slowly slipping away, by trying to bring it back, you will also start a ripple effect, as the person you are talking to will pick up on these social cues, and start using them in their conversations with others. By doing this little simple thing, you can help bring proper communication etiquette back into a trend.

Chapter 5: Additional Tips

These tips are just extra tips that you should know and insert throughout different conversations. They do not necessarily have to apply to every conversation, as they are not about the conversation itself, but how to psych yourself up to talk to people, and how to handle rejection without letting it ruin you.

Tip Seven- Get Out of Your Head

You have to get out of your own head to ever hold a good conversation with someone because you have to be able to approach someone to talk to them. If you are stuck in your head, and the "Oh I can't" thoughts, then you will be stuck at only talking to people you have to.

By getting out of your head, you will feel confident enough to approach a person that you have never met before, and that has no correlation to any of your friends. This is the best feeling, knowing that you can make friends anywhere, and not have to worry about going somewhere and not knowing anyone there.

Imagine you are going to a party. Your friend says that they will meet you there. You are glad, because you don't know anyone else who will be attending, or they are just minor acquaintances from work or school. You get there, and your friend texts you were saying that they can't come because something came up. You don't panic because you decide just to go find someone to talk to. You walk up to a guy or girl you have never seen before and strike up a conversation. Before the night is up, you have met seven new people that you really get along with.

That is what can happen once you stop the thoughts that you aren't good enough to talk to someone, or that you are too boring for anyone to want to talk to. Confidence is key. Boost yourself up, and as they say, fake it till you make it. You have to boost yourself up because there is not going to be anyone in the world who is able to make you feel better about yourself than you can. Go in with the mindset that you are worth talking to, and that you are funny and witty. By believing in yourself, people will be more open to you, as they can see that you are confident in yourself.

Tip Eight- Boost Your Self Esteem

This one goes hand in hand with getting out of your head. You have to believe in yourself to get out of your head. If you have low self-esteem, you will be more prone to rejection, because just like lions, people can pick out the ugly ones. No one wants to have to carry the entire conversation, so they generally steer away from the shy people, and gravitate to someone who they know will actively engage in conversation.

The way to boost your self-esteem can also involve a mirror. Stand in front of it for ten minutes a day only saying positive things about yourself. You are smart; you are strong, you are caring, you are kind. Do not mention any of your negative attributes. For every negative thing you say, add another minute to the time you spend looking in the mirror. It is your responsibility to build yourself up, no one else's. You can do it. As the days go on, you will find you are having to add less time onto your ten minutes, until finally, you spend just the ten minutes saying entirely positive things about yourself. Eventually, you will begin

to believe them. You are essentially retraining your brain to say nice things to you, rather than mean things.

This society is so bleak, and some so many mean people say hateful things while hiding behind a computer screen, and this has cause self-esteem rates to go way down. Build yourself back up to stay above the hatred

Tip Nine- Handle Rejection with Pride

If you have low self-esteem, this will be hard, so you have to build yourself up to be able to do this. Otherwise, it will get to you, and make you not want to talk to people any longer. If you are rejected before you build yourself up, just take some time to recuperate.

Not everyone will want to talk to you, especially nowadays. In today's age, people judge others before they even open their mouths, and decide on if a person is "worthy" of speaking to them. You have to break away from this thinking. You also cannot think that someone is above your level, they may seem like they are, and turn out to be the nicest person ever. However, when you approach someone, they may reject you, and this is okay. You may not want to talk to anyone that approaches you either.

If you are rejected, shake it off. Remind yourself that it is not you, it is who they are. They decided that they did not want to get to know you, and that is their loss, not yours. Get back up on that metaphorical horse and try again with someone else. You will find someone who is actually worth talking to.

Tip Ten- Don't Latch On

In a setting with a lot of people, it is so easy to try to find people that you enjoy talking to and staying with them a majority of the time. This is not a superb idea. You have to work for the crowd so to speak. How boring would it be if you were at a concert, and the singer only interacted with one fan? It is the same concept with talking to people. Go around to different people, and try to make more than one new friend. Eventually, you can come back to that one person, but let them have some time to talk to others, and give yourself time to talk to others as well.

How These Tips Help

These tips are for your own personal use to adapt to specific conversations and situation, and to psych yourself up before you go to a social event where you may not know someone that is there.

Following these tips will give you an edge on your conversations. Using these will help give you a self-esteem boost, and you will learn how to help yourself. These tips will make you a better conversationalist and a better you.

Chapter 6: After the Tips

If you have tried all of these tips, and find that you still cannot connect with people, you should try to see about getting some help with a psychiatrist. There could be some real deep-seated issues there. Talking to people is hard, but if you have tried to break out of your shell, and find yourself having panic attacks every time, you need to know what is going wrong.

There is nothing wrong with getting help either. Just as you would need to see a doctor for a physical illness, you should see a psychiatrist if your social anxiety is so bad that it is causing you to break down at the thought of talking to someone you do not know. There are a lot of resources that are at your disposal. If you are not sure a psychiatrist in your area, try talking to your average doctor, and he can help refer you to someone. The best thing about that is he is more likely to know a specialist to ensure that you are getting the best level of help that you can get.

How to know if it is more than just being shy

- • You have panic attacks regularly in social situations: This can be the sign of a serious problem. You should get it checked out, and maybe the doctor can help you figure out how to work through it in a way that is best suited to you.

- • You avoid stores during busy hours: If you would rather go without a necessity for a period of time because you do not want to visit a store during working hours as there will be too many people there, and could cause you to have a meltdown, you should see a doctor. This is serious. You cannot deny your needs. A physician can help you figure out the root of the problem, and set you on your way to healing.

•   •   If you feel physically ill in social situations where there are only a handful of people: If being in small groups makes you feel physically ill, you should definitely look into it. Doing so allows you to truly live your life to the fullest, once you figure out what is wrong.

Don't let anxiety control your life any longer. Get the help you deserve and do not feel bad for doing so. You deserve to live a happy life unrestrained by anxiety. Regain control of your life.

PART V

CHAPTER 1

WHAT ARE THESE SECRET KEYS TO A

RELATIONSHIP BREAKTHROUGH?

Have you ever wondered why so many people fail in their relationship with men, whether as friends or more than that? Wondered why so many couples break up, even though it seemed like they would be together forever? Do you have a hard time connecting with men enough to take your relationship to the highest level possible? Many people do, and that is because they do not know about these secret keys for a breakthrough.

It is essential to know what men want and need, otherwise, you will not be able to know him as well as you wish you could, and the distance will make it hard to connect. A connection is important when in a relationship, as it is what determines the amount of passion you have years down the road. A weak connection makes for weak passion and limited intimacy once the honeymoon phase is over.

If you do not have passion and intimacy in a marriage, this can be a major problem, as they are what keep the love alive, and the marriage

interesting. Without any interest in your marriage, it can cause many problems, including divorce, and infidelity.

So to avoid these issues you must learn about the secret keys, for without them you will be destined to have an average relationship, rather than a superb relationship. Which an average one can last forever, but a superb relationship will most definitely last forever.

Only about twenty percent of people know about these keys to a man's heart. They are the couples that you see that are eighty years old and still acting like young lovers. They are the couples that everyone aspires to be. These people are the happiest couples alive because they learned the secret keys to marriage, and to unlock their man's heart.

Why it is Pertinent to Know these Keys

These keys are the basis of obtaining a strong and intimate relationship. Almost everyone's goal in life is to get married, and have that marriage last forever. They want to be the couple that everyone looks up to, and that everyone comes to for advice.

That is where these keys come in. They are designed to help you achieve that level of a relationship in your life. These are from a man's

perspective, to help you understand more what they really want. Not what women say they want.

A man's heart is unique. It is unlike a woman's heart in many ways, and should be treated as such. You should want to know exactly how to open his heart to show you exactly how he wants to be loved.

Men are also stubborn at times. You may have already won his heart, but he has put up walls to try to prevent himself from falling. You have to break through these walls as well, which if you use these keys, should be easier than just whacking away at it with charm. Read on to find these keys.

Chapter 2:

Secret Key #1

Desire

Men do not say this aloud, which is why this key is such a big secret, but men love romance. They want their partners to put in a little romantic effort as well. This key is important, as without it, a man cannot be sure if you are really down for him or not. If he doesn't feel like you desire him, he will not completely open up to you. Very few couples realize how important this is, and that is why often times, you see relationships fizzle out so fast. Follow this key to strengthen your bond with the male species.

Romance

Describe your most romantic fantasy. Is it elaborate? Or simple? Either way, you most likely still have one. So does he. Men are romantic creatures by nature, but they also like to be romanced. Take him out to dinner, and pick up the check. Take him out to the movies, and pay for him. Return the favor he probably often shows you quite frequently.

It doesn't even have to be that expensive either. When he has a long day at work, surprise him with his favorite dinner served by candlelight. In his day off, pack a picnic lunch, and drive to his favorite spot and enjoy a picnic. It doesn't have to always be fancy, you just need to put in as much effort into showing him you want him, as he does for you.

It is about feeling wanted, and loved. If you aren't putting in an effort to show him how much you care, how is he going to know that you are going to be there in the long run? He will feel like you are only there for what he can do for you, not what you can do together, and he will begin to feel used. Value a man. Don't expect to get treated like royalty if you are only going to treat him like a peasant.

To understand more about being romantic for a guy, this scenario will help you to understand more, that it isn't always about the big things, sometimes even the smallest gesture means the world to a guy.

Scenario

James looked over at his girlfriend, and wondered if she truly loved him. She said it all the time, but how did he know for sure? Was she just fronting to get his money or was she truly his ride or die chick? How could he be sure that she really loved him?

"Babe?" He called over to MaryBeth

"Yes, baby?" She replied

"Answer three questions for me. What is my favorite color? What was my favorite memory as a child? What is my favorite food?" James needed to know if she loved him as much as he loved her. He knew that her favorite color was purple, because it reminded her of the twilight hours when everything is quiet and still. He knew that her favorite childhood memory was when her dad took some free bikes and pieced them together to make her very first bike because they were too poor to buy a new one. He knew that her favorite food was Italian, and that it only became so when she met him, because he was Italian, and showed her how real cuisine was created, rather than restaurants that order frozen food and heat it up in a microwave. He wanted to see if she knew the answers to those questions.

"You don't have a favorite color, per say. You are color blind. You say that your favorite color would be emerald green because that is the color I told you my eyes were. Your favorite childhood memory was when you and your brother climbed the big oak tree in your backyard together, and talked about life and what your plans were for your futures. You said that was the first time you two had really ever bonded,

and that was when you realized you wanted to be a real estate investor. You were nine. Your favorite food is Chinese, because it reminds you of when your mother used to take you to a Chinese restaurant every Friday for mother-son bonding time. The last time you did that with her was two days before she died. You used to dislike Chinese food, but went because she loved it, but after she died, the memories made you love it." She answered. "Now tell me. What is this about?"

"I was wondering if you loved me. No girl has ever paid enough attention to me, and focused mainly on my wallet. You answered every question perfectly. The first one to ever do so. I love you so much."

"How could you doubt I love you, James? I may not have a lot of money, but I try to show you every day that I love you. You should think about that, rather than focusing on little questions that anyone who pays attention to you could answer." MaryBeth replied, slightly offended that he felt she didn't love him.

As she walked out of the room, James sat and thought about what she said. He thought back over the course of their relationship, and thought about all the things she did for him regularly.

She cooks me dinner on a regular basis. When I have had a hard day, she rubs my back. Even though she is on her feet for over eight hours a day, and mine is just stress of a tenant not wanting to pay rent. She shows up on my longer days with my favorite meal, and we eat it together before we have to go back to work. For no reason at all, she told me to get in the car, and we drove to our favorite spot with some fast food, and ate while watching the trains pull into the station.

She always tells me she loves me before she goes to bed, even if she is angry with me. She never fails to ask me how my day was, and truly listen to the answer. Even though sometimes I tune her out when she talks about hers. I don't know what her favorite song is, or when her first heartbreak happened, but she sure as hell know mine. What have I done for her? I know the answer to three questions that anyone with half a brain could answer, and I buy her stuff. I take her out to fancy dinners, and spend money on her but that is about it, and yet she never questions my love for her. I want to marry this woman. She is my everything. She has a piece of me that no one else ever will. She truly has my heart.

James walked back into the bedroom, where he found MaryBeth crying.

He sat beside her, and began to rub her back.

"I'm sorry. I am so sorry I ever doubted your love for me. I know I could say that every other girlfriend has only wanted my money, and it broke me, but in truth; I am just an ass. I love you, MaryBeth. I want to

marry you someday. Not today, we still have a lot of things to work through, but if you forgive me, I promise that one day you will have an engagement ring on your finger." James said, pulling out a little ring and sliding it on her ring finger. "Do you accept my promise?"

"Yes. I forgive you as well." MaryBeth said, beaming with happiness while her eyes were still brimming with tears.

Discussion

James didn't realize until it was brought to his attention, all the little things that MaryBeth does for him to show her love. Sometimes you do have to give him a little wake up call to show him that you do play the romance card on a regular basis. Maybe do a big gesture here and there to really show him you care. But sometimes it just takes you telling him to think that gets his brain in gear. Be romantic, and even if he doesn't realize it at first, he will start to see all the little things you do for him, even when he doesn't notice you doing them.

Desire

You have to ignite a white-hot passion in him that makes him want to take you right here and right now almost any where you go. This desire is what fuels the passion in your relationship. If there is no passion,

things get stale, and that is when people drift apart the most. If the bedroom isn't rocking, you better get packing, because you need a good sex life, and desire filled relationship to last for a long time.

How do you ignite this desire in him? It is simple. You have to desire him as well. Men are easily enticed, if you are willing to tap into your animalistic nature. You have to want to make him desire you, so that means you will have to be pro-active in your sexuality, and prove your prowess in the bedroom, along with outside the bedroom.

How is this done exactly? Ditch the missionary position. This is the bane of all sexual existence. There are so many more positions out there, where you don't have to lie there like a lifeless doll and take what he is giving you. (Ditch standard doggy style for gay couples. This is the missionary in the gay world.) Look up new positions and try them for yourselves. Try different styles. There are some that can spice up the bedroom if you are both willing to try it.

• • BDSM: This is a type of sexual style that requires one partner to be dominant, and one partner to be submissive. Start out slow. Don't go "Fifty Shades of Grey" level the first day. Ease into it. Find out the limitations your bodies can handle, how
tight you like the collars and ties, what you absolutely do not

like, and so on and so forth. Knowing what you like is important, as if you don't like it, the experience will not be fun. Both of you have to be vocal if you want to know what each other likes and don't like. Also, come up with a safe word to use, so in the heat of the moment, you don't hurt yourselves.

• • Roleplay: This is one for when you want to experience what it is like to have sex with someone different, yet still wanting that sex to be with your partner. You get little costumes, and you dress up as someone else. While dressed up as another person, you literally become that person. You are not yourself, you are a whole other person. This could mean you have your guy become the cable guy, or you become his secretary. There are many other people you can take on the role of, such as famous people, or make up your own personas. If you do not feel comfortable with role play, but are still intrigued by it, try it on a small

154

scale. Have him be a fake person you make up, and vice versa. This will get you more comfortable with the idea, so you can more enjoy it.

• • Making a Home Video: This can be a very good bonding experience in the bedroom, as you can watch back the video

you make, and see how much you were enjoying the sex. Once you both realize how good things are in the bedroom, you will never want to leave. Relax and enjoy it, though. Don't try to put on a show just because you are being filmed. You aren't a porn star, and neither is he. Just enjoy it. You can also see what positions work for you, and what doesn't when you play the video back. These videos should never be put on the internet, or used for any other reason than your viewing pleasure. If handled correctly, they can make for great material to get you in the mood as well.

• • Watch Porn Together: This can give you an idea on positions to try, and also get you in the mood to do the deed. Find a video that you both like, and settle in. You can also try a bit of self stimulation while watching the video, but be careful not to distract yourself, or your partner from the video itself. The whole point is to learn new positions and bond. Remember though, porn is an act. Do not expect to have super explosive orgasms the first time you try a position. You most likely will have to practice a few times for it to even feel good.

There are many ways to spark up some interest in the bedroom, but how do you make him want to do these things? How do you spark the carnal desire in him? How do you show him you want him so bad it makes your stomach do flips? There are a few ways that are fool proof.

•   •   Send Him Little Notes: You can leave sticky notes all over the house for him, in his car, in his lunchbox if he has one. You can also text him all the things you would like to do to him. Tell him that you aren't wearing any underwear or something like that. Give him something to want later that night.

•   •   Tease Him: Kiss him seductively in the hall way and then keep moving along. Rub your rear against his junk, and then walk away. Play footsie with him when you eat dinner. Make him desire you, turn him on, but then leave him hanging. At the end of the night he will want you so bad, he will do anything to have you.

•   •   Be Playful: Sometimes the biggest turn on is when you act like a kid. Being free-spirited can be the biggest turn on for guys, because they like knowing you are happy and having fun. Tickle him, and then make him chase you to the bedroom and tackle you on the bed. Play wrestle a little bit, and watch the playing turn into sex real fast. Sometimes the best foreplay, is to simply play.

You have to create a white-hot desire in the pit of his stomach, one that makes him crave you when you are away, and not want to leave your side when you are near. You have to make him think about you constantly, to the point where he doesn't even want you to go to the restroom because that means being away from you for too long.

This desire will unlock the part of his heart that makes him want to commit. He won't want to leave, because he is too devoted to you, and he loves you way too much to walk away from everything you have together. You have to keep this desire alive, and strong, to keep the relationship strong and healthy.

Here is a scenario that should help you get a mental picture of what that desire looks like. Caution. This one is mildly graphic, but if you are an adult reading this, as the disclaimer warns, you have probably read much worse.

Scenario

He wanted her. He wanted her more than he has ever wanted anyone. The way she teased him drove him insane. It was like she took pleasure in keeping him aroused to the point of pain. She would pay for it, when she finally let him have her. These thoughts swirled around Mason's brain, and left him winded. He thought back to when they first met.

Lacy wasn't like a lot of girls. That is what attracted Mason to her. He was tired of girls throwing themselves at him. He was tired of girls who had nothing more to offer than a loose vagina, and some amateur head. These women bored Mason, so he never kept them around much longer than a night. Lacy, however, showed very little interest in Mason when they first met. She looked him up and down, offered her hand in a professional manner, and said it was nice to meet him. Like she was at a job interview. She didn't blush, or swoon, or make any indication that she found Mason attractive. He had to have her. She was exactly what he wanted. A challenging woman.

He became more and more infatuated with her as the night drew on, and he listened to her talk, and engaged in conversation with her. She was Harvard educated, and it showed. She wasn't haughty or anything, really she was very humble, but when she spoke her words were eloquent and well thought out. She didn't use 'like' in between every word, as most girls tend to do. Instead, every word out of her mouth was carefully planted like she was speaking a puzzle.

She turned him on. Plain, and simple. He had to have a date with her.

"Excuse me, Lacy? I am enamored by your eloquence, and would love to talk to you more, one-on-one. Would you care to have a cup of coffee with me after this party is over?" Mason asked

"Why don't we leave right now? I feel I am boring everyone else." Lacy said

"I highly doubt you are boring anyone, but if you wish, I would love to go at once."

They left the club, and walked down the street to a little coffee shop that was open twenty four hours a day. This was one of Mason's spots to think, and he wanted Lacy to experience it as well. When they walked in, he could tell that she was star-struck with the place. It wasn't well known, but it was cozy. He offered to buy her coffee, but she refused, stating that she was glad to have an excuse to leave the club.

"I hope you don't think that I am like other girls, Mason." Lacy said as soon as the found a cozy nook to sit down.

"I beg you are pardon?" Mason nearly choked on his latte

"I don't put out on the first date. You have to win my heart. You can't just bring me to a quaint little coffee shop, and expect me to sleep with you tonight." Lacy was blunt with what she spoke, there was no beating around the bush.

"Of course I don't think you are like other girls. In fact, I have never brought a woman here before."

As if on cue, the shop owner came out then to greet Mason.

"Mason, my old friend. Are you enjoying your evening? Oh! You have a lady with you! Forgive me for interrupting, I have never seen this before. Enjoy yourselves." The shop owner ducked back into his office with a bright red face.

"Well I guess I don't need to ask you to prove that you have never brought a woman here."

They sat and talked the night away. In the wee hours of the morning, Mason drove Lacy home, as her friends had already left the club.

"Lacy, can I see you again?" Mason asked, as she stepped out of the car.

"I would like that very much."

Three months later, Lacy practically lived with him. They often slept in the same bed. And he still had not been able to make love to her. That is what he wanted. He didn't want to just have sex with her, he wanted to make love to her.

"What is on your mind, Mace?" Lacy asked, sitting on his lap.

"I want you, Lacy. More than I have ever wanted anyone. I love you. I truly love you. I want to make passionate love to you, in a way no man ever has. I want to give you the world, if you will let me. You are the one I want. Forever."

"Mason, that is what I have been wanting to hear since we met. Tonight you will finally get what you want. Me."

That night was the most mind blowing night of Mason's life. Lacy felt perfect for him. They didn't leave the bedroom for hours. Everything was perfect.

Flash forward two years later, and Lacy still teased him. He still wanted her as much as he did from day one. He couldn't imagine life with any other woman, as she was the only one who lit such a desire in him.

Discussion

Lacy made Mason desire her, by not always being readily available. She let him know she was into him, but she did not give up everything from the beginning, and even after she gave it all up, she still kept that playfulness up in the relationship, making him want her bad enough to always desire her.

This is what you have to do in a relationship. You have to keep your partner interested in you. Don't think that just because you have been together for a long time, that means you have to act like an old couple. Be playful. Show each other how much you care.

Chapter 3:

Secret Key #2

Make Him Feel Safe

Men will never admit that they need to feel safe in a relationship. This key is a secret, because society makes men feel that they have to be macho all the time. This is the furthest from the truth, and you should not believe this, as everyone needs to feel safe. Not just physically, but emotionally.

Couples that know this often have less fights, and less time spent angry at each other. Fights and arguments do not stem from someone doing something that you don't agree with, they stem from being afraid that they are going to leave you. You get angry because you don't feel safe, and you are scared you are going to be left alone, so you throw up a wall. Men do the same thing as everyone else. Only they will never admit that is why they have a wall up.

You have to make him want to take all of his walls down and be open with you. Make him feel like you want to know everything about him. Not just where he grew up, what his favorite color is, and what music does he like. Ask him if he ever sucked his thumb, did he have a teddy bear or a blankie? What was his favorite television show growing up? Has he ever been in trouble? What are his aspirations, and fears? Ask him about his nightmares. Do not be satisfied with one word answers. Give him information about you every time he divulges something about himself.

Emotional Safety

You have to be his safety net as he is free-falling into love with you, just as he has to be yours. You have to catch each other, and you can't fall if you don't trust the other person with your heart. Be open always. You can't expect him to open up to you when you won't open up to him. It is a give and take relationship, when you want to unlock the part of his heart he holds dearest to him.

To make him feel emotionally safe, you have to let him know that you won't let him down. This often means listening to him talk about things you aren't necessarily interested in.

A man has to be able to cry around you to feel truly and completely safe in a relationship. Sometimes you have to assure him that it is okay to cry. Hold him when you see him having a weak moment, and let him know that sometimes even the strongest mountain breaks down. If he can't cry around you, he won't be truly open to you. Men are at their most vulnerable moments in life when they break down in front of someone, because they are bred to believe that crying means you are weak. So if a man finally cries in front of you, you have won his heart.

Here is a scenario of how to know if you make him feel emotionally safe.

Scenario

Josh loved his boyfriend very much, but he felt as if Alex was still closed off. Josh was definitely the more feminine of the two, so he was very open with Alex. Alex however, often changed the subject when it came to his past. Josh knew that Alex loved him, he just wasn't ready to completely open up. Josh was understanding, and never pushed, but still let his love know that he was there for him.

One day, Alex came home in a horrible mood. Josh didn't know what was wrong, but he ran up and hugged Alex anyway.

"Oh, baby, I can just tell you had a horrible day. Would you like to talk about it?" Josh asked.

"Actually I would like that very much, babe." Alex said with a tight throat.

"Come sit down darling, let me make you your favorite tea while you compose your thoughts."

Josh hurried off to the kitchen, while Alex sat down on the couch, looking lost and forlorn. Josh's hear broke just looking at how sad his love looked. After the tea finished brewing, Josh hurried back into the living room, and handed Alex his tea, made just the way he liked it.

"What happened love?" Josh asked gently.

"I guess there is no sense in beating around the bush. My brother is dead. He was shot in the head last night in a drug deal gone wrong." Alex said

"I am so sorry love. I didn't know you had a brother, but I am heartbroken for you nonetheless." Josh said, wrapping his arms around Alex.

"I didn't talk about him much because I was ashamed of him. He was a drug addict. He was always asking when he could meet you, and I always made excuses. I feel horrible now, because he was the only one who supported me when I came out as gay. My parents kicked me out, and he gave me a place to stay. He was the only family I had, and I judged him for something he had about as much control over as I do being gay." Alex broke down in tears.

Josh sat there and held Alex, his heart breaking for him, as it also beamed with love, because Alex was finally opening up to him. He was sad that Alex's only true family was dead, but happy that Alex trusted him enough to tell him everything. His heart swelled with love for the man in his arms crying his eyes out.

Discussion

Alex was very closed off when it came to talking about his past, because it hurt to much to talk about, and he didn't want to cry in front of Josh, and Josh felt distanced from Alex due to his wall he threw up. Once Alex finally started talking about himself, Josh knew that Alex truly loved him, and that he trusted him finally. This gave Josh a happy feeling, even in the midst of a sad time, which allowed him to truly comfort Alex in his moment of need.

Why Do You Need This Key Again?

This key is essential in opening up an intense bond between you and your partner. When you feel comfortable enough to be completely open with each other, you learn more about the other than you could ever imagine. This is important, because to truly love someone, you have to truly know them. Once you truly know everything about someone, loving them becomes a whole lot easier.

Chapter 4:

Secret Key #3

Respect and Compassion

What is the one thing that anyone wants more than anything in the world? That is right, respect. Respect is rated the number one thing that a person wants in life. It is even more of a priority than love, because you can't have love if you don't have respect.

Respect is what makes the world go round. Think Aretha Franklin. R-E-S-P-E-C-T. This song is about how just a little respect can make a world of difference. You have to respect your partner not only as your partner, but as a human being as well. You can't expect them to be perfect, and you have to respect that sometimes they have to make mistakes.

This is where compassion comes in. When your partner makes a mistake, it is always important to show them compassion and understanding. This way they know that you care enough to help them make it through the mistakes they have made.

Why is this a Secret Key?

Most people do not know that men need more respect and compassion in the relationship. Men are often more insecure then women, they are just better at hiding it. Respect and compassion assure him that you love him and care about him, and that he is good enough for you. If he feels that he is worthy of you, he will become the most devoted person you have ever met. This key unlocks the section in his heart tied to fidelity. If he feels worthy of you, he will do anything to stay there. If he does not feel worthy of you, he will look for someone who makes him feel worthy.

EGO

This all boils down to ego. A man's ego is a powerful thing. Sometimes, if not treated properly, he can become borderline narcissistic. If he feels that he is not getting the respect he deserves, he will look to get it in any way he can. This is where a lot of severe relationship problems stem from. Emotional abuse, physical abuse, infidelity. This is all a problem created when a man is beaten down. Not necessarily by you, but by the world. This is what causes people to split up, and can ruin what seemed to be a perfect relationship.

Men aren't always aware of their ego issues, so they can't tell you what they need. That is not to excuse a man who becomes abusive or a cheater, or even to say that a man is helpless. They know right from wrong, they just don't realize what is causing them to do wrong. If he is abusive or a cheater, then you should leave. No questions asked. Leave. However, if he is just being angry for no reason, maybe you aren't showing each other enough respect and compassion.

How to Show Him Respect

• • Be there for him: If he has a gig, or something important, go with him. Even if you aren't interested. Being there for him, and respecting him enough to support him shows him how much you care. If he needs you to listen to him, do so. Let him rant on about something you don't care about, but pay attention. Just because you don't care doesn't give you a free pass to ignore him or tune him out.

• • Respect His Privacy: Trust is a big thing in a relationship. Both parties need their privacy on some things, and breaking that privacy is saying that you don't trust your partner enough to give him space. A big thing that a lot of women do is go through his phone. If you can't trust him enough to leave his phone alone, you probably shouldn't be in a relationship. You also shouldn't snoop through his drawers or his personal things. Let him have his privacy, just as you want yours.

• • Respect His Personal Space: You don't have to be together every free moment you both have. Sometimes, spending time apart when you have free time is a good thing. You can do your own thing, and don't have to worry about if the other person is having fun. Men need this personal space to unwind after a hard day. Women do as well, but we are focusing on men here. If he doesn't text you back immediately, he is probably in the shower or taking a nice hot bubble bath. It does NOT mean he is cheating on you. Let him have his space without worrying about him stepping out on you. If you trust and respect him, he most likely will not want to do anything to break that trust. But if you don't trust him, he might just give you a reason not to.

• • Respect the Fact that He is Human: Men are not robots, and they are not slaves. He has needs, and he needs them tended to at times as well. You cannot expect him to wait on you hand and foot, yet not turn around to do the same for him. Also he will mess up. Don't hang it over his head for the rest of his life. Get through it, and then get over it.

Those are some ways that you can show that you respect him. Men are easy to please, and as they do not have the hormone fluxes that women do, it is more straightforward, but you still have to dig a little to find out his needs. He will give you what you need, if you respect him enough to let him.

Compassion

Compassion is important for when he is having a hard day or makes a mistake. You have to be willing to be compassionate towards someone to ever make a relationship work. Compassion is the difference between healing his heart and breaking it. If you are compassionate, he will trust you with things he doesn't trust anyone else with.

How to Be Compassionate

- - Take Care of Him: If he is having a bad day, cook for him. Clean for him. Rub his back and cuddle him. I know this new-age mentality is that women are not a man's slave and that he can do for himself. That may be true, but sometimes you have to take care of him. In return, he will take care of you.

- - Be Understanding: Men are human, and they will mess up. Don't overreact if he buys they wrong type of toilet paper, or the wrong grade of milk. They don't always get everything right. You have probably messed up sometimes as well. Did he freak out over the little things? Relax. If he isn't out killing people, or cheating on you, then discuss it calmly on why you prefer things a different way, and then make like Elsa and 'Let it Go'.

- - Don't Ridicule Him: If he is not as advanced as you in some areas, do not make him feel bad for it. If you can read the best, and he can do math the best, combine your strengths. Don't make him feel like less of a person because he can't do what you can. Don't tell him he needs to get better. If he wants to, then help him, but don't tell him he has to.

•   •   Listen to His Problems: The best thing you can ever do is just listen when he wants to talk. Not only will you learn some new things, but you will show him that you are invested in him, and by showing him a little compassion, you make him feel like he is important.

This scenario will show you how respect and compassion can help save a relationship.

Scenario

Rachel was worried about Rick. He had been acting distant lately, and was gone a lot. He always hid his phone and wouldn't let her touch it. Everyone said that he was probably cheating, but she trusted him to have a good reason for all of these things. She didn't want to be let down again by another man.

I will have a talk with him when he gets home tonight. I will ask him why he has been acting this way.

Suddenly she heard a phone ring. She checked her pockets, but it wasn't hers. She investigated the sound, and found her boyfriend's phone behind the toilet. There was a strange number calling.

Should I answer it? No. I trust him. It is probably just a telemarketer, and his phone probably fell behind the toilet this morning, and he didn't grab it cause he was running late to work.

Rachel knew that Rick would be home in a few hours, so she busied herself with errands and cleaning the house up. Five o'clock rolled by, and Rick still wasn't home. She started to get worried, and with no way to contact him, she couldn't allay her fears. But she told herself to remain calm, and that he would show up.

Finally, around seven o'clock, Rick came walking in the door. Rachel flung herself into his arms because she was so worried. Then she noticed that he didn't smell like the fiberglass mill, and he was surprisingly clean for being at work all day.

"Rick. We really need to talk." Rachel whispered, on the verge of tears.

"What's wrong?" Rick asked her

"I have been trusting of you, and I still trust you to tell me what is going on. I am trying not to assume you are cheating. However it is really hard to think of any other explanation why you have been coming home late, hiding your phone behind the toilet and getting strange calls. I didn't answer it by the way. Your clothes are too clean to

be coming out of the fiberglass company, and they are the same clothes you walked out of here wearing. You don't smell like you normally do after work. Please just tell me what is going on." Rachel burst into tears.

"Oh Rach." Rick sighed, pulling her into his arms. "I got laid off a couple of weeks ago, and have been looking for a job ever since. That number was probably a job calling so I have to call back tomorrow. I'm late because I have been doing odd jobs to continue making enough money to support us, so you don't have to. I wanted to tell you, I just didn't want you to worry."

"That is what this is all about? You knew I was cheated on several times by my last guy, and you leave me worrying that it is happening again? Babe, I would have understood if you had told me, and I would have supported you, and even got a job myself if need be. I love you, and I want you to tell me about your problems. Please don't hide something like this again."

"Oh Rachel, I love you so much, and I didn't realize how bad it looked. I am so sorry, and I promise to always tell you about these things from now on." Rick said, kissing Rachel passionately.

Discussion

Rachel could have jumped to conclusions and accused Rick of cheating on her, thus making him angry for her not trusting him. However, she decided to ask him about it and listen to what he had to say. She was understanding when he told her what was going on, and let him know she wanted him to bring his troubles to her, even if it meant that he had to put some stress on her. She wanted to take on these problems together.

By being compassionate, and respecting him enough to trust him, she avoided what could have been a really big fight. Instead they were brought closer together, as they opened up with what was bothering them.

Why is this Key Important Again?

You have to respect each other to get anywhere in a relationship. Without respect you have nothing, and you can't truly love someone if you do not respect them. Compassion is needed to ensure that your relationship is not a miserable one. You have to respond with compassion to avoid having an argument blown out of proportion. People are not robots or dolls, they will mess up.

You have to use this key to unlock the part of a man's heart that trusts you. He doesn't open it up for just anyone. Most men do not trust half of the people they say are close to them. They could not be vulerable to these people. You have to unlock that for yourself.

Chapter 5:

Secret Key #3

Be Confident

Men do not want to be with a woman who is always questioning if she is good enough for him. They want a woman who knows her worth. Men want to know they are with someone who feels valued. If you aren't confident, it makes his job of making you feel secure that much harder. He feels he always has to lift your self esteem, and that can be a hard job for anyone.

Confidence is not always just knowing you are worthy of love, however. It is also taking care of yourself. Taking care of your personal hygiene and keeping yourself groomed. You do not have to be perfect, just put an effort into keeping yourself clean and well kept.

Most people don't realize that this is important in a relationship, and that is what makes it a secret key. It is important to use this to unlock his desires for you if you are looking to start a relationship with him, and you must remain confident and well kept to unlock his never waning desires for you.

Confidence

Everyone has their insecurities, there is no doubt about that. However it is important to not let your insecurities rule your life. You can have some things that make you not so sure about yourself, but you have to be able to work through them.

Confidence is important in any aspect of your life, but it is certainly important in relationships. Not only do you have to be confident in yourself, you have to be confident in your relationship as well. You can't expect a relationship to thrive if you don't have any confidence in it. You have to believe that it will succeed, and that you are good enough for it to succeed.

In this scenario, you will learn more about what poor confidence can do to a relationship.

Scenario

Blake was super insecure. He constantly doubted himself, and if he was good enough for his boyfriend Michael. Michael hated that Blake was so insecure, and wished he could see how gorgeous he was. It caused many fights, because Blake felt that he wasn't good enough and did everything in his power to make Michael see that. Which included picking fights for no reason at all.

I wish I was confident enough to make this relationship work. I am just not good enough for him. He is perfect, and I am a fat lard. I really need to lose weight. I am so fat. Why does he stay with me? Can't he see I'm a disaster?

These are the thoughts that went through Blake's head daily. He couldn't ever get close to Michael, because he was scared that Michael would see that he was a disaster. He constantly had a wall up that Michael was trying to break down.

I'm exhausted. Blake never lets me in, and I'm am so tired of trying to break through the walls he puts up. I wish he could see how much he means to me. He is perfect just the way he is, if only he would stop worrying so much.

Michael was tired of always trying to boost Blake's self esteem, so with a heavy heart, he broke up with Blake.

"I told you I wasn't good enough!" Blake screamed, with tears in his eyes.

"You imbecile! That is the reason I am breaking up with you! You don't feel like you are good enough for me, and I am tired of you ignoring every effort I make to try to show you otherwise! You are perfect just the way you are, and I wish I could have made you see that! I don't want to leave, but I can't keep breaking my heart when you won't let me into yours!" Michael yelled back.

"So you aren't breaking up with me because I'm not breaking up with you, you are merely breaking up with me because I feel like I am not?" Blake whispered

"Yes. I want nothing more than to be with you, but I have to think of my own emotional health as well."

"What if I promised to get help for my insecurities? Would you stay with me? I love you Michael, I just don't want to be hurt anymore. I want you to love me too."

"I do love you Blake, and if you actively get help, then yes, I will stay. But you have two weeks to show me you are trying." Michael said, embracing Blake.

Discussion

Blake's insecurities almost cost him the love of his life. He was so worried about Michael pushing him away, that he didn't realize he was the one doing the pushing. Blake was not confident in himself, and it was tiresome for Michael to always be the one to supply the confidence for the both of them. Michael felt like Blake couldn't truly love him, because he never let him in. It almost destroyed their relationship beyond repair.

If Blake had realized that Michael wanted to be with him for who he was, he would have avoided this whole scene, and been very happy. Let your confidence shine through. You may not feel confident, but fake it until you make it. If you seem confident, you will start to feel confident.

Take Care of Yourself

Men want women to be healthy. This does not mean that you have to eat organic food, and wear full face makeup every day of your life. Just shower regularly, and keep yourself groomed. If you are a slob, and unhygienic, most men will feel that is a sign of lack of confidence, and they will stay away from you. You have to make yourself appear to be ready for a relationship to find the right relationship. If you look like

you don't care about yourself you are going to attract someone who doesn't care about you as well.

If you are in a relationship, and start letting yourself go, you will make your man feel like you don't care about the relationship as much as you used to. (This doesn't count if you have kids. Though you should still try to shower regularly) You should always want to keep your hygiene up regardless of your relationship status.

Why is this Key Important?

This key unlocks a man's desire for you. Human's primal instinct is to mate, and men are really close to their primal instincts. He will be looking for a strong woman suitable for carrying his children, so that his offspring are strong and successful. By being confident, and taking care of yourself, you attract men that will value you, and treat you well. If you are not confident, and do not take care of yourself, you often will attract losers and abusers.

Chapter 6:

Secret Key #5

Give and Take on the Lead

This key is one of the most secret keys there are, because most people don't realize that the man doesn't always wear the pants in a relationship. You both have to make the big decisions together, and take turns on the smaller ones. You cannot let one single person take control of the relationship. If you work together, you unlock a bond that allows him to see you as an equal and not as below him.

If you make all of the decisions in the relationship, you allow him to be passive, but if he makes all the decisions, you become passive. Neither one of you should become passive, because this is a one way ticket to a controlling relationship. While it does not always end up that way, fifty

six percent of relationships where one person is in charge of most or all of the decisions turn into be abusive relationships.

The solution to avoid this problem is to take turns making decisions. Even the smaller decisions like where to go when you go out to eat, or what to watch on television. On the bigger decisions, make them together. Especially on whether or not to buy a house or start a family, or any big purchase.

Also, take care of finances together, or split them up equally. You cannot give one person complete control of the finances, and expect to not have some control issues. Money is the biggest player in a controlling relationship. If one person has all the control of the money, they can tell the other partner what they can and cannot do, and once you get a taste of that power, it escalates from there.

The best way to avoid this is to get a joint account if you are married that has both of your names on it, so you both can access the funds, or have separate accounts with only your name on it, so the other partner can't access the funds. If you do this though, you have to decide how to split the bills. Otherwise, there will be issues with bills not getting paid, and utilities being shut off. This is if you live together. If not, you don't have to worry about it.

If you don't want to take turns on even the little decisions, then work together to decide everything. From where you want to eat, to where you want to live. Working together will create a strong bond between you two as well. You will grow closer together as you achieve things together. Think about it. If you make great strides in your life with the one you love, who are you going to celebrate with? That's right, them. So it only makes sense that if you make all your decisions together, you will grow closer due to the fact that you celebrate every achievement as one. You have to want to work together though, otherwise, you will argue more than you work together.

Why is this Key Important?

You want to unlock his heart in a way that makes him see you as an equal rather than a lesser, as society tries to make everyone think. If he sees you as his equal, he will learn to depend on you, rather than walk all over you. There will be less debates on who should make what decisions, and who is always right, because you will both be able to compromise and work together to achieve a blissful relationship.

PART VI

CHAPTER 1

WHAT DO YOU WANT?

Do you walk into an electronics store or a car dealership without knowing what you want? No, if you are like most men, you buy magazines that tell you all the technical specs about the latest technology and cars. You also go online to forums and tech websites to do research.

Why would you try to pick up women or try dating sites without knowing what you want? You do not want to do that. If you are like most men, then you have dated, enjoyed one-night stands, and explored the pool of women.

Now, you are reading this book because you are looking for something more. Perhaps, you haven't dated more than a few women and wonder what you are doing wrong?

The men who are successful in relationships, who find those long term marriages—they are the ones who know what they want.

I'll give you an example of a marriage that lasted 42 years. It would have lasted longer if illness did not exist. This couple met when the wife

moved into a new apartment complex with two other female friends. The young man, at the time, came up to see if there was anyone he wanted to date or would want to go on dates with him.

He would call up the night he wanted to date and see if someone was willing. He even spent eight months in another state. But, this man realized he had met the one person for him in that apartment.

He came back from living in a different place with one thing in mind— to ensure this woman would date him. He tried his nonchalant style, calling up the day of to ask for a date. She would always refuse because she also had other plans already in the works.

Finally, this man asked, "what do I have to do to get you to go out with me?"

The answer was simple, "call in advance."

The couple dated a few times before Christmas, every week during January and were engaged the day before Valentines.

Life doesn't always happen this way, but you can be sure that the man knew what he wanted. He dated several women, going out when they were available, and enjoying coffee, a meal, or a movie. But, no one caught his attention as much as the woman he married. It took distance to realize that no other woman compared.

If you have not dated very many people, then you need to get out there. You need to start dating more. How else are you supposed to figure out what you want?

I'll give you another example. This couple was together for 17 years and married for 13, almost 14 years. The marriage ended with a divorce and two suffering children. The man dated only two people, marrying the second. The woman had dated more men, but also enjoyed being the center of attention, the person that knows it all, and the person who lies because she doesn't recognize the truth. When the husband asked her father for her hand, the father said, "she is just like her mother, are you sure you know what you are doing?" Her mother constantly spends every dime that is earned, is all about herself, and often depressed and unhappy. Of course, the husband thought he could live with it all, only to find that the woman he was marrying could easily ask for a divorce and immediately move in with another man.

The lesson in this second example is—you can know what you want and what you are capable of living with, but you also have to make allowances for the other person.

A person who cannot love themselves will never be able to love another with their whole heart.

Are you willing to accept being second or loved with less than a whole heart? Are you willing to date or marry someone when, you know, eventually, it will come to an end, it's just a matter of how long it takes? These are the questions you need to ask yourself as you begin to learn the secrets to enter a woman's heart completely. Only when you know yourself and what you are willing to accept, can you truly find your way into the right woman's heart.

CHAPTER 2

SECRET KEY #1

Open, Honest, Consistent Communication

Pick up a woman's magazine that has a quiz. I bet that quiz has a section on communication. It probably tests the woman on how communicative her partner is and offers advice on how to elicit more communication. There are millions of these quizzes and articles in magazines, online, and they are all designed for woman by woman. Yet, you can learn something from this concept. Why do you think communication is such a hot topic? It is because women are fundamentally different from men.

Women can be extremely intuitive, even read body language, but women still consider the way men think a mystery. Women cannot believe a man is only thinking about sex. There has to be something more in your brains, right? You are capable of multitasking at your job, of dating multiple women, and holding deep conversations on politics, religion, engineering or something equally complicated—so you must have more on your mind than sex.

You also have feelings. These feelings can be hurt. You can also be excited and feel love. Women are unable to understand why you are unable to talk about these deeper feelings, and demand that you do.

A group of women get together and they catch up. What has happened in your life, what are you doing now, what happened last week. The conversation invariably turns to emotions, but it is not the whole discussion.
Women seek other women for emotional support and understanding because they feel they lack it from the men in their life. Women also work on hormones more so than men.

It's a fact and not something you should fear discussing. A woman can be happy one moment and the wrong words can flip a switch. The grudge can be held for days with the wrong words. A man usually forgets about the issue in a few hours or days, unless the same thing keeps happening.

So, on one hand, women have a need to know your emotions because they cannot understand them unless you tell them. On the other, there are emotional mind fields that you have to navigate as you communicate.

It has been the experience of most women that men do not want to communicate about their feelings. They find it a waste of time. Yet, it is the one thing that will help your woman feel confident in the relationship. It is the way for you to work your way into their heart. The key is for this communication to be open, honest and consistent.

Defining Open

What does open communication mean? In business, it is a setting where employees are encouraged to share their thoughts and concerns, without the fear of retaliation (reference.com). In a relationship, it is the same thing, only the thoughts and concerns to be shared are about personal situations.

Communication includes issues about one's job, the treatment of the person by their boss, monetary concerns, kids, religion, love, and all other feelings people have.

For example, a family of four sat around a dinner table to discuss whether a move to a new state would be the best option for their family. The discussion included the changes that would occur, the employment options for the parents, and why the move would offer monetary stability versus the current place they lived. Each person was given a chance to discuss their thoughts, fears, concerns, and acceptance of the move.

Another family of four also moved. In this family, the parents sat their children down, said they were moving, and stated where. No communication from the children was allowed as to how they felt or why a move had to occur.

Do you think the children in the first family were more prepared and less unsettled than the second family? Of course, they were. They weighed in with their opinion, fears, concerns, and desires. The second family's children had to keep what they thought to themselves.

Now, consider this example, as a communication between two people: You have two people in a relationship, where one person is always stating what is going to happen, without giving reasons or why it is the best? How unsettled will the partner be? How angry do you think they will become at not having a choice?

Open communication is required to help your woman understand how you think, the reasons behind your actions, and to feel secure in the relationship. If you do not share your thoughts and feelings, how are they to know what you are really thinking? How are they to feel secure that you truly care about them, if they are not kept in the loop or considered part of the equation.

The game telephone provides a good example of this concept. One person starts a statement and by the end of ten or twenty people the statement has changed drastically. By the time your body signals based on your emotions are translated by a woman, they are changed because she is going to interpret them based on how she thinks, just like you try to interpret her behavior based on how you think.

Without communication, you are unable to figure out what each of you is thinking.

Honest Communication

Does this outfit make me look fat? Yes. Ouch. But, it is also how you deliver the answer. You need to be honest because there is one thing a woman does not want—she doesn't want to wear something that does not look good and she will feel embarrassed about later on. Also, here is the kicker—if you lie about how she looks in an outfit—what else could you be lying about?

It is far better to tell the truth when asked for it, then to lie. Furthermore, it is 100% better to speak the truth in any situation. If there is a behavior that bothers you, speak up. One woman told her husband this, "If I start acting like my mother, tell me." She was fearful that she would start displaying certain negative behavior that her mother had and she didn't want to. She was always hurt when being told "you are acting like your mother," but it also helped her realize that a correction to her behavior was required.

A woman who loves herself and gives of herself, completely, to the man she loves is capable of accepting the truth. The anger and stewing for a few hours is better than ignoring the problem or lying to avoid conflict.

Now will all women agree, no. Some women are unable to take the hurt that honest communication provides, but ask yourself, do you want a woman who can give her whole heart because she values your honesty or the woman who keeps a grudge and eventually causes too much pain?

You want the woman who can give her whole heart, so be honest in your communication and explain why you will always tell the truth, even if it is not what the person wants to hear. You'll be valued for this

behavior because you are noticing and trying, as well as remaining truthful.

Consistency

More times than I have fingers I have seen relationships start where each person is honest, and communicative. However, after a year or two, the communication stops being consistent. It is like each man and woman believe they have figured the person out and know what they are thinking, so it is less necessary to be communicative. Wrong.

You cannot become complacent just because it seems like the woman is not demanding communication as often as she was. There are only a few reasons she feels communication is no longer as necessary:

- • She thinks she knows you well enough that she can read your moods.

- • She is no longer interested.

- • She is angry when you don't truly communicate.

If it is the first, then you need to show her that talking each night before you go to sleep is important to you. You need to give of yourself for her to continue giving of herself.

If she is no longer interested, you need to know, so you can move on to find the right person. Sometimes a woman has just as much difficulty breaking off a relationship. She doesn't want to cause hurt when she is unwilling to give her whole heart.

The last reason is fairly easy to discern. If you have not provided any worthwhile communication, then she will turn away, say "fine, whatever," or something along those words and stop trying to communicate with you. For communication to unlock your woman's heart, you need to:

- • Learn to read body language

- • Read the subtle nuances in her tone

- • And give of yourself before you ask her to give of herself

If you are embarrassed about your thoughts because they are just about "sex" in that moment—don't be. Tell her. But more than anything, have a time of day when the two of you talk about what happened at work, the challenges or the good things, and plans that you have or things that you want to do.

The conversation does not have to be deep and always about emotions each night. Rather, you are supposed to come together, be honest, be consistent, and just share. You are not to judge, just to listen, with attentiveness. If you only hear the words, then you cannot repeat them. Here is something else that is usually a complaint from a guy, "all she has ever said are complaints. We never talk about anything other than how much she hates this or that."

Did you ever think that perhaps she is not happy with something that could be changed? Perhaps she needs a new perspective? Maybe, feelings of unhappiness in other areas of her life are making her complain about something else? The biggest one—did you ever think that she only communicates when there is something negative?

Try it, if you are already in a relationship. Track your communication for a week. Did your woman want to talk when she was happy or did she only want to talk when something was bothering her? Did you try to get her to talk about her day or the happy stuff, or did you think "yay, I don't have to try communicating today?"

Your effort to get her to talk when she is happy, will be rewarded. She will know that she can talk about anything, but more that you care to listen about everything. She will learn to talk about the good and the bad, so you don't hear only the unhappy things.

Thus, the ultimate secret is your effort in getting her to communicate about all things, just as much as she is asking you to communicate about anything at all.

One man said, "I didn't think you wanted to listen. I figured it would bore you."
His statement was definitely an insight into why he lacked communication. It was also the key his partner needed to understand that she needed to put more effort into listening.

Most try to say that communication is a two-way street, but is it really? If you drive on a two-way street, you have to keep to your own lane to avoid an accident. I suppose you could "meet in the middle," and block traffic. I'd rather think of communication as a one-way street. One of you has to be illegally driving to meet in the middle, but sometimes that is what it takes for a heart to open. If you are not willing to put in the effort to circumvent any blocks in the way, such as illegally driving down a one-way street, then how can you open up her heart?
She will see the motivation and honesty in your effort to communicate on all subjects that are important to you and her, not just what may be important to her. This will open her heart a little further, and allow her to trust in your feelings for her.

CHAPTER 3

SECRET KEY #2

Equality and Respect

This is a chapter that should be common sense, but more often than not, it is not. Countries were founded on inequality and there are many still struggling with inequality issues to the point that women are killed if they step out of line. Given how sensitive a topic this is—it should not surprise you that all women want to be treated equally and with respect.

Yes, there are people with more intellect than others, but talking down to them or disrespecting them is not the proper way to communicate. What if you were faced with a woman who had an IQ of 185 and she consistently talked down to you even about simple topics? A man's pride gets pricked pretty easy. It is annoying when a woman is or acts smarter than you. So, why wouldn't it be annoying and insensitive if you are always acting smarter than the woman you are with.

Here is an example: A young man not very well versed in subtle body language and common sense would talk about simple things, a topic that he had in common with a young woman. But, he would often use an arrogant tone with an "I know more than

you" attitude. He would tell this young woman things she already knew, like she didn't know the first thing about it.

The relationship didn't last. Nor will any relationship in this situation, when the woman is capable of knowing herself, her own intellect, and a proper way of having a conversation.

It doesn't have to always be about conversation, either. It is just an easy example that helps shore up the previous chapter.

When you communicate in a relationship, the woman wants to be seen as your equal, to have an equal opinion. She doesn't want her words discounted because you know better.

She wants her words to resonate, for you to think about them, and help explain why something else would be better or why her opinion is valued, but not the right approach.

For example, let's say you are married and you have a child. Your child starts to refuse to eat. You might have a different viewpoint than your wife. Your wife might allow the child to go to bed without food until the child finally figures out that starving is not the answer. You might not want your child to go to bed hungry, so you will allow your child to choose a healthy snack such as apples and cheese.

Your wife feels that you are giving in to your child and their refusal to eat healthy things. You might feel that letting your child go hungry, can have unhealthy consequences. Who is right or wrong? That is not the answer. The question is who is going to see results quicker? If the father will get the child to eat healthy foods, then the child will remain healthy. If the child continues to not eat enough, even with healthy snacks then this can hinder the path to a solution. Whereas, starving often gets a child to eat, even a little of something they don't like or a willingness to try it cooked a different way in order to never go to bed hungry again.

The debate won't be answered here because the point is not to solve the question, but to realize that if you refuse to listen to your partner's opinion, harm could be done in more ways than one. You could end up hurting your child and on the other hand, you are putting your wife in a position of disrespect in front of the child.

Dismissing what your partner, whether you are dating, going to the next step, or married, is not going to get her to open her heart to you. Are you always right 100% of the time in all areas? Of course not, and neither is your partner.

The key is for you two to be able to see each other as equals. You look at each other, know your strengths and weaknesses, and compromise when necessary, but never with a disrespectful attitude.

It is okay to point out certain mistakes, but make sure you do it with respect. Value the person and they will open their heart to you. They will also value you more, for showing that you value them.

If you have not yet noticed this is leading to "trust." For a woman to give their entire heart to you—they need to trust you, trust that you understand them, respect them, and value what they have to say or to give in the relationship.

Communication is not the only way to make this known. Body language is also very important in a woman being seen as an equal. If you ignore something they say or do, it is an act of disrespect, of seeing them as less.

For you it may be complacency. You might be used to the person always cooking your dinner, so you forget to say thank you or take notice of their hard work. The husband or boyfriend who is successful never lets anything go unnoticed.

Car Doors and Other Doors

"She has her own hands; she can open the door."

Have you ever thought this? Perhaps you know someone who has? Maybe, the women you have dated told you it is unnecessary to open doors for her?

Yes, a woman likes to do for herself, but that doesn't mean you should never open a door for her. Choose your moments. Make it a surprise. Even a woman who is capable and willing to open her own doors, appreciates when a gentleman will do it for her. It is based on when you open the door.

For instance, let's say your girlfriend has her arms full of things and there is no hand to open the door. You would immediately open it for her, right? Of course.

The next time you need to open the door is when you are taking her out for a special dinner.

"Let me get the door." This statement tells her that you appreciate that she is coming with you and that she has dressed lovely for the evening. It is a "special" occasion that supersedes the usual rule that she will open her own doors.

If you are running late and it is easier for your partner to open her door, then wait and she doesn't mind opening her own door—it is okay to let her. If she is the type that always needs the door open as a sign of chivalry, then you still, have to open it.

It is not about the door. It is about the effort and respect such an action provides. Again, you let the woman make a choice based on her preferences or you simply ask what she prefers. You choose your moments to be sweet or you always show respect because that is what your heart tells you to do.

There are men who will tell a woman, "I was raised to open doors as a sign of respect. Not complying with this, goes against the respect I have for you."

The key again is to communicate what you know to be right, so that your partner also understands your point of view.

You should back down to show your respect, but also in the same light tell her that you are respecting her more by following through with certain instincts.

Remember these suggestions are examples. You have your upbringing and your partner will have hers. As long as you show mutual respect for each other, and equality of the minds, then you will have a woman who is willing to show you her heart.

CHAPTER 4

SECRET KEY #3

Acceptance for Who They Are

What is the one thing many women have tried to do when they started dating you? They tried to change you. The wrong woman always tries to change her partner. They want you to fit into an ideal they have for a man. There are plenty of reasons for this.

- • She is afraid of never finding someone who will accept her

- • She feels you are broken and in need of fixing

The two bullet points are the two main reasons she may try to change you. A smart woman will eventually realize that she cannot change the man she is dating. She has to accept him for who he is, his faults and strengths, or find someone else.

You may wish to change the woman you are dating too. Perhaps she doesn't care enough about her appearance? Maybe, she shops and spends too much money? It may be something simple that you do not like, but cannot seem to ignore.

You have an option. You can stop dating a person because she has habits or traits you cannot ignore or you can accept them. It is your choice, but you need to make it.

Don't stay with someone because of your own fear. Yes, men do have fears. There are men out there who fear that they will have to settle for one woman because the one they want is unattainable. Did you ever think that you are not settling, but finding the person who is right for you? Do not settle if things do not feel right and in the same vain do not choose a woman who you cannot accept for her faults and strengths.

If you already have problems or fights due to basic personality clashes, then you are not going to get the woman to stay with you and give her full heart.

The secret is to truly accept, no matter what or to realize that you cannot. If you can accept all of her faults, then you will open her heart a little more, and eventually her whole heart will be yours.

The one thing you cannot do is change your mind and expect her to open her heart. She has to know that there is consistency within your own heart. You either accept her for who she is or you don't. If you do not really accept her faults, then you will always have doubts in your mind. You will always question or find yourself focusing on the things you cannot accept. People can only change themselves if they see a problem. They are not going to change because you want the change to happen. For a time, they may try to be better, but after a while, their inherent traits will win out. There is no way around the traits winning, unless the person they are a part of is willing to change.

Yes, you received an example earlier that stated the wife wanted to know when she was acting like her mother. The key here is that she wanted to know. She asked for the truth. She was already in the frame of mind that she may need to change her behavior if she became like her mother.

If you try to point out things to a woman who has not asked or does not think there is something wrong within herself, then you are not going to succeed. She will close her heart and doubt that you can love her fully when you cannot accept all of who she is.

There is also a difference in accepting who a woman is and being her support for the changes that she wishes to make.

What if the woman you are dating had a bad family experience as a child? What if she lacks confidence? Can you deal with her frame of mind and self-doubt? What if you could be her support to help her build her self-confidence without actually pointing out that she needs the help?

It is possible. If you are open and willing to accept the woman for who she is and the potential of who she desires to be, then you are going to find her whole heart is in your hands.

By now you should see a theme in the secrets to a woman's heart: trust and support.

Any woman you date needs to feel they can trust you and that you will be supportive. Without trust and support, she is going to feel like you are only partially in the relationship and she is going to hold back.

It does not matter how many relationships you have had that reach the next level from dating casually to steadily. It does not matter if you have married before and your marriage has failed or is struggling. If you can provide trust and support for the woman you value in your life, you will finally succeed in opening her complete heart to you.

The Pedestal

One man succeeded and another did not. There was a time when one woman was dating two men. She would go out on Fridays with one guy and Saturdays with the other. Both men knew she was dating someone else, but they had never met. One man asked for her hand and was given a "yes." The other took her to a wrestling match the day she received the marriage proposal. The next date he found out she was going to marry the other guy and asked, "are you sure. I love you, you are everything to me, I've put you on a pedestal and don't know how I can live without you being my wife."

The woman's answer: "Your first mistake was putting me on a pedestal." No one wants to be on a pedestal.

Already it was mentioned that you need to accept the woman for who she is. A part of this discussion is about that very concept. You do need to accept a woman's faults.

More importantly, you cannot raise a woman too higher than she truly is. You cannot have a "celebrity" image of the woman you wish to date.

What if every woman went around trying to find her perfect guy from the romance novels she reads or the songs that have been sung?

You know she won't find this guy because you know men have faults and are not romantic heroes like in the books and movies.

You cannot put a woman on a pedestal and expect a life of happiness to follow.

The minute you put a woman on a pedestal is the minute your relationship is wrong.

You have to be supportive and help her learn to trust you, but you cannot make her a "goddess," in your mind.

Do not keep the rose colored glasses on and reference what you truly want. What do you wish to see in a woman you can spend your life with? Are you the type of man who needs space, but will never stray? Can you look at attractive women, but know that the one beside you, is the most attractive because of the entire package? If so, then you don't need a pedestal for her. You just need to marry her if you haven't already.

CHAPTER 5

SECRET KEY #4

The Pedestal

One man succeeded and another did not. There was a time when one woman was dating two men. She would go out on Fridays with one guy and Saturdays with the other. Both men knew she was dating someone else, but they had never met. One man asked for her hand and was given a "yes." The other took her to a wrestling match the day she received the marriage proposal. The next date he found out she was going to marry the other guy and asked, "are you sure. I love you, you are everything to me, I've put you on a pedestal and don't know how I can live without you being my wife."

The woman's answer: "Your first mistake was putting me on a pedestal."

No one wants to be on a pedestal.

Already it was mentioned that you need to accept the woman for who she is. A part of this discussion is about that very concept. You do need to accept a woman's faults.

More importantly, you cannot raise a woman too higher than she truly is. You cannot have a "celebrity" image of the woman you wish to date.

What if every woman went around trying to find her perfect guy from the romance novels she reads or the songs that have been sung?

You know she won't find this guy because you know men have faults and are not romantic heroes like in the books and movies.

You cannot put a woman on a pedestal and expect a life of happiness to follow.

The minute you put a woman on a pedestal is the minute your relationship is wrong.

You have to be supportive and help her learn to trust you, but you cannot make her a "goddess," in your mind.

Do not keep the rose colored glasses on and reference what you truly want.

What do you wish to see in a woman you can spend your life with? Are you the type of man who needs space, but will never stray? Can you look at attractive women, but know that the one beside you, is the most attractive because of the entire package? If so, then you don't need a pedestal for her. You just need to marry her if you haven't already.

CHAPTER 6

SECRET KEY #5

Make Her Smile

The key to most women's hearts is to make her smile and laugh. The right woman will accept your personality, whether it is sarcastic humor or witty humor. It is also the effort you provide in making her smile or laugh. For example, a coworker recently knew his female coworker was having a bad day. They are friends and nothing more, as there is a significant difference in age. Yet, the man, going through his own trials, still worked for a good hour to make her laugh and smile rather than to continue crying as she was doing.

This is a man who understands that humor, even in making silly faces, giving out zinger, witty remarks, is the key to making a woman fall a little in love, even if it is only friendship.

You don't have to be the wittiest. You may have a stupid joke that makes one groan more than laugh or smile. However, the effort in trying to make the woman smile, to make her laugh, will instantly make her heart melt.

Gifts are Important

Surprise gifts are important to a woman. They consider these gifts as supportive or endearing because you are paying attention to her. There are times when life gets routine, mundane, and even filled with complacency on both of your sides. The trick is to come home with a surprise.

Flowers are nice for some women. For others, they are an instant allergy issue. Some men feel that flowers are going to die, so why spend the money, when something else can be provided, such as a vacation from saving money on the little things.

The key is to know what your woman believes and what you can do that will matter to her heart. Sometimes it can be the silliest thing or the simplest. What if you both love tattoos? Did you ever think about getting a tattoo of a symbol or date that matters to both of you?

Perhaps, it is as simple as coming home with a card. Maybe when she goes on a business trip you hide a card in her bag moments before you say goodbye at the airport.

Gifts do not have to be expensive, they do not have to be jewelry, but they do need to be thought of and given. Yes, some women prefer expensive gifts, even demand them, and if you have a wife or partner like this, then you need to comply sometimes. It goes back to accepting and knowing the woman you have in your life. However, it doesn't mean that small things like cards and spontaneous gifts that are not expensive won't move her heart.

It is all about what you know about her desires, what she is used to, and what will make her smile and love you because of the effort you have shown. You can also show a woman used to expensive gifts that it is not the money, but the honesty behind the gift that matters the most.

CHAPTER 7

Special Bonus Tips

Not all women will fit your personality. There are some women who should not be in relationships or marry, unless they can find a partner who is just like them in the key ways. There are even some women who will never open their heart and find true happiness because they cannot find it in themselves. These bonus tips will help you look at relationships and women, so you might succeed, when you have faced certain issues such as being in a bad relationship, failing to be supportive in small ways, or even noticing her each and every day.

Things to Look Out For

- • Does your current partner feel love is shown through how much you buy her?

- • Does she flirt with other men to see if you are getting angry or noticing what she is doing?

- • Does she seem to pick a fight or get angry for no reason you can see?

- • Has she started to withdraw from you?

- • Is she starting to ignore you, your phone calls, or breaking dates?

These are a few signs that you need to look out for in understanding that she is not the woman for you. Some of these can also be a sign that she may have a psychological issue that she cannot get passed and will eventually affect the relationship.

For instance, have you ever date a woman who lies, who tries to separate you from friends and family, needs "things" to feel you love her, and is always thinking about herself? This can be the sign of a narcissist. A narcissist is someone who views themselves as the most important, cannot handle when someone else is more important, is often arrogant, and knows everything. This same person also blames

everyone around them for being at fault and for doing things they are actually doing.

Toxic relationships like this need to be avoided, even if you feel you can live with this person's faults. Drama is another word that has been applied to women who seem to cause conflict, always pick a fight, and have a healthy sexual appetite that never seems satisfied with just one person.

Only you can truly say what type of relationship you are looking for, but there are definitely signs that you need to watch out for with regards to women and drama they can create.

- A woman can call you several times a day or demand that you call them often.

- They may ask where you were and not trust your answer.

- They may text or try to start up a conversation that is too deep on the first meeting.

- They may complain and find nothing happy.

These are just a few other signs that a woman may not be right for you or perhaps anyone. Someone who is obsessive without actually dating you can have psychological issues that require a professional. It may not

be nice to say of one's own sex, but it is also the truth. Some women need to recognize their failings and accept those in order to find a healthy relationship, otherwise they are "crazy" in their actions towards men, bordering on obsessive.

Signs of a Wrong Relationship

Relationships do not have to be filled with "crazy" or drama to be wrong for you. There are definite signs that a woman is not right for you, when she is unwilling to give her heart to you. It is not a matter of you trying harder to be supportive, and not complacent in the relationship.

Here is an example of a woman. See if you can see why she might be wrong for a relationship with you.

- • She prefers her own company to others.

- • She has social anxiety.

• • She needs a routine and does not like that routine to be interrupted.

• • She is hyper-organized, hating when someone fills up a space she just cleaned.

• • She cannot trust easily.

• • She is unwilling to be hurt and face the loss of a husband, preferring to die before any of her family, so she doesn't have to face that horrible situation.

• • She also has a dislike of touch, something no one can pinpoint a cause for, but one that holds her from a deep physical relationship.

Obviously, this is an extreme example, but take note of it. Sometimes the signs are subtle and other times there is a big sign saying "this is not right." A woman who does not allow physical contact after three dates either has issues with physical contact or does not see you as a sexual partner. A relationship that is not right for you will have fights, ups and downs, and disagreements on the main issues. You won't be able to agree on politics, religion, children, and life in general.

Additional Effort Options

A couple was having trouble in their marriage. The wife was unhappy. The man knew it, but couldn't figure out what to do. He decided he would ask her each morning, "what can I do to make your day better?" At first, his wife thought he was being insensitive and joking. After he kept asking she realized that he meant it and started answering, as well as asking how she could make his day better.

Such a simple phrase and the care behind it saved the marriage. You can do something like this in your relationship. It doesn't have to be a big deal. It can be something as simple as asking how your partner's day was or how you can make it better.

It can also be something that will make her smile. The married couple of 42 years is another great example. One child was grown, married, and nearing having children. The second child left home to live 3,000 miles away. Living as just the two of them, the wife was missing her children. To make her day better, the husband took one of the stuffed animals his daughter left when she moved away, and started creating funny scenes.

One day the orangutan stuffed animal was holding a fake cigarette and reading in their bed. The next day it was playing chess with one of the wife's stuffed bears of similar size. For over a week, the husband would wake up, create a scene, leave for work, and his wife would come home to it. She would smile. Now she has pictures of these scenes to help her memory, since the husband passed away from early onset dementia. These little efforts changed the wife's outlook for the day, the ache in her heart from missing her daughter, and now is a comfort to her with him gone.

What can you think to do that would have such a lasting impact because it is guaranteed to open the woman's heart for life.

Flowers are acceptable, of course, and even desired by most women. But, if you have the imagination, find something that can truly make her smile, laugh, or even cry with happiness. It matters.

Helping Your Partner become a Better Her

The couple who spent 42 years together respected each other, loved each other, and were best friends as well as husband and wife. One of the biggest impacts the husband had on his wife, was mutual respect, equality, and the power to give her what made her a better version of herself. This is not about changing the person, but giving her the tools to go after what she desires.

The wife was told by her mother on more than one occasion that she was stupid, worthless and that her mother wished she had never been born. Her only choice of work was to go to a trade school. Given the year she graduated, her only real choice was to become a hairdresser. It was not something she hated, but her husband also gave her the choice of being able to do more and spend more time with her children as they grew.

In fact, she started working with her husband on construction sites building houses as a family. It gave her more freedom to spend with her

children, as well as spend every day with her husband. When she would ask can "I do this or do that," such as take ballet, he told her "you never have to ask. You can do what you want to do."

He gave her the power to try different things and be who she was, without judgement. It helped that they had the money for her to try new things, but all the same he told her they were equal that the money they made was hers to spend as she wished.

Now, she was also brought up in a poor family, so spending money was a difficult decision. She never spent money that was earmarked for bills, groceries, and necessary monthly expenses. She was responsible in the spending, but also given the chance to explore and do.

It made her heart open more for this husband. You may find that you are drawn to such a woman yourself. You also need to realize that while she is becoming a better version of herself because of you, she can also make you a better version of yourself. It is not about changing who you are inherently, but about taking what you are, loving who you are, and helping you be the best you can be even in the face of adversity.

The person who can allow this and accept such help in return is the person that can form a long term, lasting relationship with the right woman. It is also the person who will have the whole heart of the woman he loves.

Withholding Due to Fear

A lack of support and trust in a relationship can lead to the woman you are dating or married to, fearing to give her whole heart to you. There are subtle signs you need to look for if the woman fears giving her heart.

- • She will withhold herself too.

- • She will often go on trips without you for business or to visit family, and not call.

- • She will test to see if she can live without you.

- • She will test you in communication to be more open in conversation.

- • She will become angry or distant if you answer wrong or continue to withhold.

- - More fights will occur.

- - She will start to ask where you see the relationship going.

These are fear tests that she is giving you. She is hoping that you will realize her fear and start to open up, start to pay attention, and show her through action not words, how much she means to you.

If she is not the right woman, then don't let her live in fear. If she is the woman you wish to gain her whole heart, recognize the fear, address it, and start changing how you communicate, offer her your trust, and support.

What do you do if a woman says she is moving out? Do you let her or do you ask her what is going on?

If you have established open communication, where she feels she can trust you, but is not receiving proper support or respect, she will tell you her fear. If you have done nothing to gain her trust, respect, support, or communication she will be evasive and tell you "it's just not working or it's me not you."

For the right woman, you will strive to correct yourself to make her more comfortable and recognize your fault and the fear of the relationship she is feeling. If you cannot give her that, then you need to allow the relationship to end, learn from it, and start looking for the woman who is right for you.

Are you Clinging

There are certain turn offs for a woman.

- • She does not want to be your mother.

- • She does not want to constantly clean up after you.

- • She does not want to cook you every meal you eat.

- • She wants you to make an effort.

- • She does not want you to call 10 times a day.

•   •   She wants you to respect what she says and remember what she says.

•   •   If she tells you no, then it is no. Not maybe, not flirting, not suggestive.

•   •   If she asks for your opinion or a decision on what you want to do—give her one.

•   •   A woman wants a decisive man, who knows himself, and is not afraid to laugh at himself.

Above all she does not want a man who clings. She does not want someone who is obtuse to her feelings or the subtle information she is giving him. She wants someone who is willing to pay attention, to be supportive, who will try to gain her trust, and love her so she can open her heart to him.

CPSIA information can be obtained
at www.ICGtesting.com
Printed in the USA
LVHW080501090621
689775LV00024B/374